ADHD

Titles in the Diseases and Disorders series include:

DISEASES & DISORDERS

ADHD

Barbara Sheen

LUCENT BOOKS

A part of Gale, Cengage Learning

Detroit • New York • San Francisco • New Haven, Conn • Waterville, Maine • London

LIBRARY OF CONGRESS CATALOGING-IN-PUBLICATION DATA

Sheen, Barbara.
  ADHD / by Barbara Sheen.
    p. cm. -- (Diseases and disorders)
  Includes bibliographical references and index.
  ISBN 978-1-4205-0142-1 (hardcover)
  1. Attention-deficit hyperactivity disorder--Juvenile literature. I. Title.
  RJ506.H9S538 2009
  618.92'8589--dc22

                                                              2009013454

Lucent Books
27500 Drake Rd.
Farmington Hills, MI 48331

ISBN-13: 978-1-4205-0142-1
ISBN-10: 1-4205-0142-9

Printed in the United States of America
1 2 3 4 5 6 7 13 12 11 10 09

Table of Contents

"The Most Difficult Puzzles Ever Devised"

Charles Best, one of the pioneers in the search for a cure for diabetes, once explained what it is about medical research that intrigued him so. "It's not just the gratification of knowing one is helping people," he confided, "although that probably is a more heroic and selfless motivation. Those feelings may enter in, but truly, what I find best is the feeling of going toe to toe with nature, of trying to solve the most difficult puzzles ever devised. The answers are there somewhere, those keys that will solve the puzzle and make the patient well. But how will those keys be found?"

Since the dawn of civilization, nothing has so puzzled people—and often frightened them, as well—as the onset of illness in a body or mind that had seemed healthy before. A seizure, the inability of a heart to pump, the sudden deterioration of muscle tone in a small child—being unable to reverse such conditions or even to understand why they occur was unspeakably frustrating to healers. Even before there were names for such conditions, even before they were understood at all, each was a reminder of how complex the human body was, and how vulnerable.

While our grappling with understanding diseases has been frustrating at times, it has also provided some of humankind's most heroic accomplishments. Alexander Fleming's accidental discovery in 1928 of a mold that could be turned into penicillin has resulted in the saving of untold millions of lives. The isolation of the enzyme insulin has reversed what was once a death sentence for anyone with diabetes. There have been great strides in combating conditions for which there is not yet a cure, too. Medicines can help AIDS patients live longer, diagnostic tools such as mammography and ultrasounds can help doctors find tumors while they are treatable, and laser surgery techniques have made the most intricate, minute operations routine.

This "toe-to-toe" competition with diseases and disorders is even more remarkable when seen in a historical continuum. An astonishing amount of progress has been made in a very short time. Just two hundred years ago, the existence of germs as a cause of some diseases was unknown. In fact, it was less than 150 years ago that a British surgeon named Joseph Lister had difficulty persuading his fellow doctors that washing their hands before delivering a baby might increase the chances of a healthy delivery (especially if they had just attended to a diseased patient)!

Each book in Lucent's Diseases and Disorders series explores a disease or disorder and the knowledge that has been accumulated (or discarded) by doctors through the years. Each book also examines the tools used for pinpointing a diagnosis, as well as the various means that are used to treat or cure a disease. Finally, new ideas are presented—techniques or medicines that may be on the horizon.

Frustration and disappointment are still part of medicine, for not every disease or condition can be cured or prevented. But the limitations of knowledge are being pushed outward constantly; the "most difficult puzzles ever devised" are finding challengers every day.

A Misunderstood Condition

Home design expert and television host Ty Pennington is one of over 10 million Americans with attention-deficit/hyperactivity disorder (ADHD). Until Pennington began treatment, the disorder made his life difficult. He was easily distracted, restless, and impulsive. In school his mind wandered constantly, making it hard for him to focus consistently on the task at hand. As a result, his grades were poor.

He also had trouble sitting still and behaving appropriately. He felt compelled to move around and talk out of turn, even though he knew he was not supposed to. Not surprisingly, he was labeled a troublemaker, when, in fact, he had a medical condition that made it almost impossible for him to control his own behavior.

Pennington's condition affected his personal relationships, too. It was difficult for him to focus his attention long enough to participate in conversations, and he would often blurt out inappropriate comments. His peers thought he was odd and excluded him from social activities. He felt like an outsider much of the time. "Growing up with ADHD can be a little difficult," he admits. "It's not easy to communicate with people. . . . So you become kind of alienated. You feel like you're different, and, you don't really fit in. . . . So, as someone who has had ADHD, and is overcoming it, proper treatment has truly changed my life and made an amazing difference."[1]

Ty Pennington, a television star who is known for his abundance of energy, has attention-deficit/hyperactivity disorder.

Common Complaints

ADHD is a misunderstood condition. Typical symptoms of the disorder, such as restlessness, impulsiveness, and/or inattentiveness, plague almost everyone at one time or another. What distinguishes individuals with ADHD from the rest of the population is that their symptoms are more frequent, persistent, and severe than those of other people, and they impair their lives in some way. However, because everyone exhibits ADHD-like symptoms occasionally, many individuals with ADHD spend years not knowing they have a medical condition. Friends, family, teachers, coworkers, and peers often mislabel them as lazy, willful, spacey, unintelligent, and/or disruptive because of their behavior. "My husband of the past eight years thinks I'm lazy because I can't keep a job, cook, or keep the house immaculate on a daily basis. Growing up, my mom thought the same things, as did my teachers,"[2] explains Cassy, a thirty-six-year-old woman who was recently diagnosed with ADHD.

Such labels can lead individuals with ADHD to doubt themselves. Making matters worse, when people with ADHD try to control their behavior without medical help and repeatedly fail, their belief in themselves may decrease even further. "What happens is my confidence just kept waning and waning. . . . It wasn't until I finally got treated . . . that I realized . . . I actually do have a talent . . . and I actually can make something of myself,"[3] explains Pennington.

Stereotypes and Misconceptions

Even when people with ADHD are diagnosed, they face problems. Although ADHD is a real medical condition, some misinformed individuals deny that ADHD is a real medical disorder that requires medical treatment because the symptoms are commonplace. The problems that characterize the disorder, they insist, can be overcome if individuals with ADHD try harder to control their behavior. "All through school," explains Allen, who lived with this sort of criticism most of his life, "teachers, family, and friends would all tell my parents and me 'he could be/do anything he sets his mind to.' HA! Set my mind to it. Nobody ever told me how to do that. My mind has never been set, resists being set, and in fact, has no conception of what that means whatsoever."[4]

Like any other illness, ADHD cannot be willed away. "You wouldn't tell a blind man to watch his step," says Kathy, a woman with ADHD, "but you are in fact telling us that very thing when you tell us we need to get our heads out of the clouds and pay attention!"[5]

Misconceptions that deny the seriousness of ADHD and the need to treat it keep some individuals from seeking professional help. They cause some parents of children with ADHD to feel inadequate. And, they make many who do seek treatment ashamed that they need medication to control their behavior. Maya Bolton, a woman who recently started taking medication for ADHD, explains, "I worry. If people, particularly co-workers, knew about my diagnosis, might they consider me one of the shirkers, someone who just wants an excuse for flaky behavior?"[6]

Widespread Impact

The same lack of understanding about ADHD also impacts society. Left uncontrolled, ADHD can cause a multitude of problems. A 2004 Harvard Medical School study found that more than 15 percent of adults with ADHD had abused or were dependent on alcohol or drugs within the prior year. Researchers think individuals self-medicate with these substances to soothe their ADHD symptoms. Many turn to criminal behavior to support their habit. "In high school," explains Rob Surratt, a young man with ADHD, "I was smoking pot every day after school to calm me down. I was drinking, too. . . . In senior year, I started dealing drugs."[7] Impulsivity also leads to criminal behavior, as well as unplanned pregnancies and domestic violence. Some psychiatrists estimate that as much as 90 percent of the American prison population suffers from the disorder.

Unmanaged ADHD also has a financial impact. According to noted ADHD expert Russell A. Barkley, an estimated 35 percent of individuals with the disorder drop out of high school. Without a diploma, they find it difficult to earn a decent living. Moreover, people with ADHD may have trouble holding jobs. Due to restlessness or impulsivity, they tend to switch jobs frequently.

Some people whose ADHD is left untreated may turn to drugs or alcohol to help themselves feel calm.

Such job-hopping can result in failure to get promotions and pay raises. These factors not only cause financial problems for individuals and their families, but they also impact society when these individuals turn to government programs for assistance.

Knowledge Is the Key

Educating the public about what ADHD is and what it does to individuals is the best way to destroy harmful misconceptions. It is also the best way to support patients and their families. Knowledge about the condition can help the families, friends, coworkers, and teachers of individuals with ADHD to better understand their behavior and provide them with support. It can help people with the disorder to overcome negative self-perceptions and seek the help they need. "Everyone who has [ADHD] can sculpt a fulfilling joyful life," say ADHD experts Edward M. Hallowell and John J. Ratey, both of whom have the disorder. "Doing so starts in your head. . . . You need knowledge. . . . Knowledge of what is truly going on can restore confidence and inspire hope."[8]

CHAPTER ONE

What Is ADHD?

ADHD is a complicated condition whose exact cause is unknown. The most commonly held theory is that the brains of individuals with ADHD have chemical, structural, and/or functional differences from those of people without the disorder. The cause of these differences has not been established. Because ADHD tends to run in families, scientists think that in most, but not all, cases an inherited gene (or genes) is responsible. So far, one specific gene has not been identified, but a number of genes involved with brain chemistry, structure, and function have been. Flaws in any of these genes may make individuals more susceptible to developing ADHD.

Having ADHD, according to ADHD experts Edward M. Hallowell and John J. Ratey, is

> like being supercharged all the time. . . . Your brain goes faster than the average brain. Your trouble is putting on the brakes. You get one idea, and you have to act on it, and then, what do you know, but you've got another idea before you finished up the first one, and so you go for that one, but of course a third idea intercepts the second and you just have to follow that one. . . . You have all these invisible vectors pulling you this way and that, which makes

it really hard to stay on task. Plus which, you're spilling over all the time. You're drumming your fingers, tapping your feet, humming a song, whistling, looking here, looking there, scratching, stretching, doodling.[9]

Chemical Differences

The human brain is responsible for all the body's physical, mental, and emotional functions. It is a complex organ composed of more than 100 billion cells called neurons and is divided into three large regions.

Each region of the brain is responsible for specific functions. For each region to do its job properly, neurons throughout the

Children with ADHD can be noticeably distracted, drumming their fingers or looking off into space.

The Brain

The human brain is responsible for every function of the body, including a person's personality, talents, emotions, thoughts, and perceptions of the world. The brain weighs about 3 pounds (1.4kg), making it into one of the largest organ in the body.

Brain cells called neurons make up the brain's gray matter. The neurons transmit information in the form of electrical signals along a network of fibers called dendrites and axons, which make up the brain's white matter.

Information is sent to different parts of the brain. The cerebrum is the largest part of the brain. It has two halves, or hemispheres, which comprise four lobes. The frontal lobe controls speech, movement, learning, and emotions. The parietal lobe is involved in touch and sensing pain and temperature. The occipital lobe controls vision. The temporal lobe is involved with memory and hearing.

The cerebellum is the next largest part of the brain. It controls muscle movement and balance. It transmits information up and down the spinal cord.

The brain stem is the smallest part of the brain. It is located at the base of the brain. It controls life functions such as heartbeat, breathing, circulation, and sleep.

brain must communicate with each other. Chemicals known as neurotransmitters allow this to happen. Transported on proteins along wirelike pathways, neurotransmitters carry information between the different regions of the brain. Without neurotransmitters, neurons could not communicate with each other, and the brain could not direct the body.

There are at least fifty types of neurotransmitters. Each carries different information, which controls diverse body functions or is involved with various emotional or mental functions. Two neurotransmitters, dopamine and norepinephrine, carry

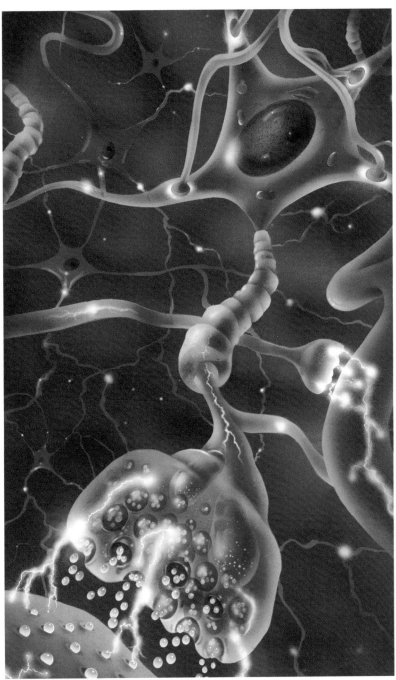

Some scientists believe that problems with the neurotransmitter dopamine (shown in blue) can result in ADHD.

information involved in attention, memory, impulsivity, self-control, organization, and activity level.

Research suggests that a chemical imbalance, which is simply an overabundance or a deficiency in one or more neurotransmitters, is at least part of the problem underlying many mental illnesses. For instance, abnormally high levels of dopamine are linked to schizophrenia and paranoia, while high levels of norepinephrine are linked to anxiety disorders. Scientists, therefore, theorize that a chemical imbalance plays a role in ADHD.

A 2007 study by the National Institute on Drug Abuse sought to prove this theory. Researchers performed brain scans on nineteen adults with ADHD and twenty-four without the disorder. They found that the adults with ADHD released less dopamine into their brain pathways than those without the disease. "Individuals with ADHD have a decreased function of the brain dopamine system. ADHD, clearly, is associated with a biochemical dysfunction,"[10] concluded researcher Nora D. Volkow. Similar studies, which examined the brains of adults with ADHD using imaging tests, yielded similar results.

Structural Differences

Other studies comparing the size and shape of the brains of people with ADHD to those without the disorder indicate that structural differences in the brains of people with ADHD may be linked to the condition. A study conducted by the National Institute of Mental Health from 1992 to 2002 compared the brains of 152 children with ADHD with 139 children of the same age and gender without the disorder (called the control group). Each child's brain was scanned two to four times over the course of the study, using magnetic resonance imaging (MRI). The researchers found that, as a group, the brains of the children with ADHD were 3 to 4 percent smaller in all regions than those of the control group. The study also showed that the children with ADHD had a lower volume of white matter in their brains than the control group. White matter in the brain contains fibers, which form the pathways that neurotransmitters travel upon. It is possible that this discrepancy could inhibit the flow of information in the brain.

Other studies have looked at differences in particular parts of the brain. Some research has found that the basal ganglia, a part of the brain involved in motor control, emotions, and learning, is asymmetrical in some people with ADHD, whereas it is symmetrical in people without the disorder.

Functional Differences

Still other studies have found functional differences in the brains of people with ADHD. A 2005 study at the Institute of Psychiatry in London, England, challenged sixteen adolescents with ADHD and twenty-one adolescents of the same age and gender without the disorder to perform a task that involved impulse control. A rapid form of MRI measured the level of activity in their brains while they were performing the task. The researchers found that the adolescents with ADHD had less brain activity in their frontal lobes, the part of the brain involved in impulse control and thought, than the control group. Other studies have yielded similar results.

It is becoming increasingly clear that something out of the ordinary is occurring in the brains of people with ADHD. Whether the cause is chemical, structural, or functional or a combination of these has not yet been established. More studies are necessary before scientists can reach a definitive conclusion.

Acquired Causes

Although scientists believe that brain differences linked to ADHD are usually caused by an inherited gene, approximately one-fifth of all ADHD cases have been linked to other causes. Although these causes are acquired, they, too, affect the brain. For example, a fetus's developing brain can be adversely affected by exposure to unhealthy substances before birth. Babies born to mothers who smoked or drank alcohol during pregnancy have a two-and-a-half times greater chance of developing ADHD than children born to mothers who did not engage in these activities.

Since brain cells continue developing throughout childhood, other causes can also lead to ADHD developing. These include a severe head injury that causes a loss of consciousness, lack

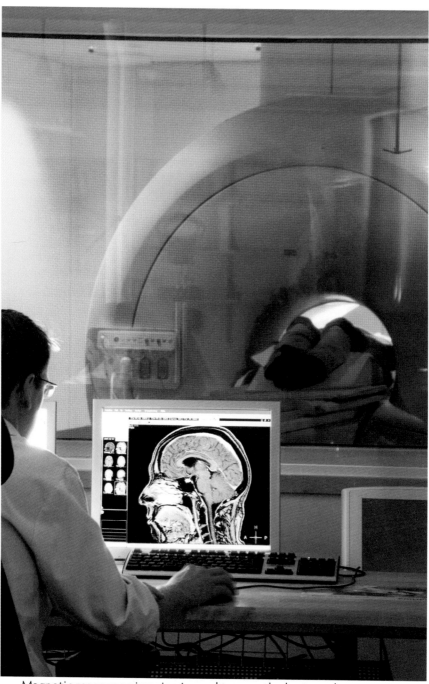

Magnetic resonance imaging is used to scan the brain and measure its level of activity.

An Interesting History

Attention-deficit/hyperactivity disorder has puzzled physicians for centuries. Its symptoms have been attributed to many causes, and it has been treated in many ways. In the Middle Ages the symptoms were believed to be caused by the devil. Prayers were said to purge the devil from patients' bodies. When this did not work, patients had holes drilled in their heads to let the devil escape.

Centuries later, in the 1800s, physicians thought that ADHD symptoms were inborn, caused by the immoral behavior of the patient's parents. Frequent beating was considered the best treatment for children with the disorder. In the 1900s ADHD symptoms were attributed to spicy food. Patients were treated with a bland diet.

By the 1940s the idea that ADHD was caused by a problem in the brain was taking hold. In the 1960s the condition was named hyperactive child syndrome. Treatment with stimulants was beginning to take hold.

The disorder was renamed attention deficit disorder in 1980. The name was finally changed to attention-deficit/hyperactivity disorder in 1994.

of oxygen to the brain as might occur in a near drowning, lead poisoning before age three, a brain tumor, or an infection in the brain.

A Condition with Many Faces

Just as ADHD appears to have a number of causes, it also appears to have a variety of symptoms. Although the condition is characterized by distractibility, inattentiveness, restlessness, and impulsivity, not every ADHD sufferer has all these symptoms. In fact, attention-deficit/hyperactivity disorder is the medical name given to three related conditions in which people have trouble regulating their behavior. Each condition has different symptoms. Scientists think that an individual's symptoms depend on specific differences in that person's brain. The American Psychiatric Association identifies three types of ADHD. They are inattentive, hyperactive/impulsive, and combination ADHD.

Inattentive ADHD

Individuals with the inattentive type of ADHD have trouble consistently focusing their attention, but have no problem with restlessness or impulse control. These individuals are easily distracted. Their minds tend to jump from subject to subject like rapidly changing channels on a television set. Jack Prey, a boy who has the inattentive type of ADHD, puts it this way: "Have you ever been working on something important, when a song pops in your head? Then that leads you to think of something in the song about flying, which leads you to play with your remote control glider? Next thing you know, it's dinnertime and you haven't finished the homework you started two hours before. For me, [ADHD] means I can't focus whenever I really need to."[11]

Such distractibility makes simple tasks like listening to a lecture, completing an assignment, following or carrying on a conversation, or reading social cues, among other things, difficult. Eighteen-year-old Rob describes how inattentiveness affects him: "When I sit down to do my homework, it takes me longer than other kids because I lose focus and have to keep making myself stay on task. When I had to take the SATs, it was hard to focus for so many hours. At school or at home, when I ask a question, I'm told 'why didn't you listen the first time?' I'm very motivated. I try to listen. But sometimes it's impossible."[12]

In addition, inattentiveness causes problems with short-term memory, organization, and time management. Maya Bolton describes how it affects her behavior:

Recently I had to cut short a telephone call to handle some urgent business. The distraction lasted only a few minutes but by the time it was over, I'd forgotten about the call. . . . This kind of disconnect is not unusual for me.

Walking around my house in the morning, I find myself narrating reminders: "Turn off the iron," or, with a slap to my forehead as I'm heading out the door, "keys." Shortly after arriving at the office, I often have to return home to retrieve a notebook or a file.[13]

Interestingly, problems with inattention do not occur all the time. People with the inattentive type of ADHD and those with the combination type of the disorder, which includes inattention among other symptoms, have the ability to hyperfocus. Hyperfocus usually occurs when an individual is performing an enjoyable activity. While hyperfocusing, individuals enter a state of extreme concentration in which they become thoroughly engrossed in an activity to the point of becoming completely unaware of time, place, or activity around them. Julia, a young artist with the inattentive type of ADHD explains, "It's like tunnel vision. I'll start working on a painting and won't stop until it's done. While I'm working, my family will be talking to me and I won't even hear them."[14] For reasons that are unclear, more females than males have the inattentive type of ADHD. Thirty percent of all ADHD cases fall into this category.

Hyperactive/Impulsive ADHD

The hyperactive/ impulsive type of ADHD is the least common form of the disorder. Nine percent of all cases of ADHD fall into this group. The dominant symptoms are restlessness and impulsivity. This type of ADHD is more common in males than females, and researchers do not know why. Individuals with hyperactive/impulsive ADHD are extremely restless, fidget a lot, talk excessively, and are usually very impatient. They have trouble taking turns and waiting in lines, may have frequent outbursts, and tend to interrupt when others are talking. Impulsiveness often leads individuals with this type of ADHD to develop risky, thrill-seeking behaviors that frequently take the form of gambling, compulsive shopping, or drug addiction. It leads them to act without considering the consequences. Impulsiveness caused Blake Taylor, a high school student with ADHD, to set fire to his kitchen. Another time, he built a giant

Children with ADHD can often seem bored or distracted in a classroom environment.

slingshot. He said, "I hit and shattered the back window of a green Cadillac." He also recalls:

> At home, I shattered the glass patio door twice with pebbles. I didn't mean to shatter the glass. At the time, I was thinking of how entertaining it would be to see flying pebbles. A person with ADHD often does not think about cause and effect, does not connect the dots between thought, action, and consequence. You shoot pebbles because you want to see them fly, and you don't think about the objects in your path. The pebbles hit the windows, people get angry, and you get yelled at. . . . These all seem like independent—and unrelated—events in your mind.[15]

Combination ADHD

A person with the combination type of ADHD has all the symptoms of the other two ADHD types, the inattentive and the hyperactive/impulsive. It is the most common form of ADHD, affecting 61 percent of all people with the disorder. It affects males more frequently than females, and researchers do not know why.

A Chronic Condition

The symptoms of all three types of ADHD usually first appear in children younger than seven. Because ADHD symptoms affect people differently at different ages, for many years experts believed that ADHD was a disorder that children outgrew. This is not usually the case. Eighty percent of people with ADHD do not outgrow it. For them, it is a chronic disorder, which means it is a lifelong ailment that cannot be cured. As these people age, however, the disorder impacts them differently. For instance, adults with ADHD appear to be less hyperactive. Instead of being outwardly restless, they often feel restless on the inside. Their hyperactivity frequently causes them to become workaholics. They tend to overschedule their time and are constantly busy.

Impulsivity in adults often appears as a volatile temper, and inattentiveness is expressed in procrastination, poor time management, and disorganization. According to ADHD expert Russell A. Barkley, "We're not seeing anything that suggests a qualitative change in the disorder. What's changing for adults is the broadening scope of the impact. Adults have more things they've got to do. We're especially seeing problems with time, with self-control, and with planning for the future and being able to persist towards goals. In adults, these are major problems."[16]

Interestingly, ADHD symptoms do disappear after puberty in 20 percent of ADHD patients. Scientists theorize that structural differences in the brains of these individuals caused them to develop ADHD. For unknown reasons, these individual's brains are slower to develop than those of other people, but they do catch up eventually. When they do, their symptoms vanish.

Associated Problems

Besides causing problems with attentiveness and/or hyperactivity and impulsivity, ADHD is often accompanied by other brain-related disorders. For instance, 20 to 40 percent of peo-

Some people with ADHD can develop impulsive, risky behaviors, such as gambling or drug addiction.

ple with ADHD have learning disabilities. A learning disability is a problem in learning that occurs in people of average or above-average intelligence despite good instruction. It is defined in the Americans with Disabilities Act as "a disorder in one or more of the basic psychological processes involved in understanding or in using language, spoken or written, that may manifest itself in an imperfect ability to listen, think, speak, read, write, spell, or do mathematical calculations."[17] Scientists do not know why such a large percentage of people with ADHD have learning disabilities. They theorize that learning disabilities are caused by functional differences in how people's brains operate. Since functional brain differences are a possible cause of ADHD, they speculate that this is the link between the conditions.

In addition, many people with ADHD develop psychiatric disorders. For example, 25 percent develop depression, 25 percent develop other mood disorders, and 58 percent develop oppositional defiant disorder. Scientists do not know why this is so. It may be that chemical imbalances are the connection between ADHD and these illnesses. Indeed, some medicines used to treat depression are also effective in treating ADHD, which points to a biochemical link. On the other hand, it may be that some people develop associated mental disorders as a response to the impact ADHD has on their lives. The frustration and feelings of failure that many individuals with ADHD experience, for instance, could lead them to develop depression.

Sleep disorders, too, often accompany ADHD. A link between sleep disorders and ADHD is not surprising, since ADHD symptoms make it hard for individuals to quiet their minds and/or their bodies. According to physician and author William Dodson, three-quarters of all adults with ADHD report being unable "to shut off my mind so I can fall asleep."[18] These people say that their thoughts race from one problem to another as soon as they turn out the lights. As a result, many people with ADHD are unable to fall asleep until the early hours of the morning. Once asleep, they tend to toss and turn. Many move around so much that they tear off their bed linens. This type of sleep is not refreshing, which may be why 80 percent of adults with ADHD say

Often a person with ADHD suffers from insomnia, the inability to fall asleep because of an overactive mind.

they have trouble waking up in the morning and are plagued with daytime sleepiness.

Individuals at Risk

Anyone can have ADHD. Certain individuals, however, are at greater risk. A family history of the disorder increases an individual's vulnerability to developing it. A 1991 study at Massachusetts General Hospital compared the families of children with and without ADHD. The study found that children with close family members, such as parents or siblings, with ADHD have a five-time greater chance of having the disorder than children who have no close relatives with the disorder. If a child has one parent with ADHD, that child's chance of having ADHD is 30 to 50 percent. If both parents have it, that number rises to above 50 percent. If a child has at least one sibling with ADHD, the child's chance of having the disorder is 32 to 41 percent. If the sibling with the disorder is an identical twin, the other twin has an 82 percent chance of also having it.

Physician Patricia Quinn explains, "I come from a family of five girls. Three of us have ADHD and my dad probably had it as well. As ADHD is often inherited, we now have a third generation with several nieces and nephews diagnosed and on medication. In my family two of my four children exhibited symptoms of hyperactivity and distractibility as preschoolers."[19]

Gender also increases a person's susceptibility to ADHD. Males are more likely to have ADHD than females. In children, three times more boys are diagnosed with the condition than girls. In adults, the ratio drops to two to one. Scientists do not know why males are more vulnerable to ADHD.

The troubling reality is that there are still many unanswered questions about ADHD. It is a complicated condition that can cause diverse and often lifelong problems for those who have it. Although anyone can develop the disorder, the risk is greater for males and those people with a family history of ADHD. Seeking medical help is the first step in managing the condition.

CHAPTER TWO

Diagnosis and Drug Treatment

Diagnosing ADHD is tricky. Once it is diagnosed, treatment with medicine can reduce symptoms but cannot cure the disorder. Moreover, ADHD medication can cause unpleasant side effects.

A Confusing Diagnosis

ADHD is difficult to diagnose with precision. Because most people exhibit ADHD-like symptoms occasionally and ADHD symptoms can range from mild to extreme, it is easy to confuse normal behavior with that of ADHD. Since most young children are typically inattentive, restless, and impulsive, diagnosing children under age five is especially hard. Not surprisingly, many people are misdiagnosed with the condition while others go through life with ADHD without ever being correctly diagnosed. ADHD experts Edward M. Hallowell and John J. Ratey estimate that 10 million adults in the United States have ADHD but only 1.5 million have been diagnosed and treated.

Adding to the problem, other psychiatric disorders share similar symptoms with ADHD. ADHD is often confused with these conditions. Illnesses such as depression, seasonal affective disorder, anxiety disorder, obsessive-compulsive disorder, conduct disorder, oppositional defiant disorder, and bipolar disorders all share ADHD-like symptoms. In fact, 70 percent of

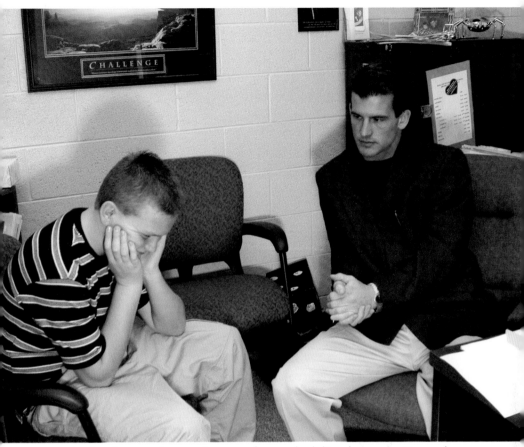

A school counselor may be one of several adults who can notice and help support kids with ADHD.

individuals diagnosed with bipolar disorder also qualify for an ADHD diagnosis. Greg, a man with ADHD, was repeatedly misdiagnosed due to this confusion. He recalls:

> The first psychiatrist that I consulted diagnosed something else. The second worked on issues suggested by the first psychiatrist. I felt that I was not getting anywhere. . . . I consulted psychiatrist number 3 whose diagnosis was that there was nothing wrong with me. "It's all in your mind," was his diagnosis. I felt I knew myself best. I felt that for my family's sake and my own sake I needed to know what made me the way I was. I felt I was at a major

juncture of my life. I considered myself a failure, but I would not give into this conviction! I did believe I needed to keep searching answers. . . . It was not until psychiatrist number 4 that I was diagnosed.[20]

Further complicating an ADHD diagnosis, medical conditions such as problems with hearing and sight can cause inattentiveness. The symptoms of an overactive thyroid gland mimic ADHD symptoms. Family problems can also produce ADHD-like symptoms. This is particularly true among individuals who are dealing with a serious problem at home, such as a divorce or a sick or abusive parent or mate. These individuals may be so worried about the future that they are unable to focus in school or at work.

Creativity and ADHD

People with ADHD score higher on tests of creativity than the general population. This may be because the impulsiveness that many people with ADHD display compels them to take creative risks and decreases their inhibitions. This makes them unafraid to try something new or something that others might consider absurd. Impulsivity also allows them to ask questions that others might be too inhibited to ask, which might be the key to new ideas and solutions to problems.

In addition, inattention, which often leads to daydreaming, may be the first step in creative undertakings such as writing or painting. Wandering attention also allows individuals to view a problem from different angles, possibly seeing answers that more focused people who follow a more logical train of thought might miss. Indeed, people with ADHD often connect facts in unique ways.

Hyperfocus also enhances the creative process. And, high energy levels allow individuals with ADHD to stick to a project for long periods while hyperfocusing.

Traits of giftedness can also be confused with ADHD. Gifted individuals often appear inattentive or restless, but their inattention and restlessness are due to boredom. Michael Kearney, a highly gifted boy who graduated from college at age ten, was misdiagnosed with ADHD when he was a toddler due to inattentiveness. His parents did not believe ADHD was the source of his problem. "Children like Michael have an attention surplus. He is so much faster than we are. In two seconds, he's figured out what you are going to say. He's toyed with a few answers and now he's looking around waiting for you to finish. It looks like he's not paying attention,"[21] his father explains.

No Conclusive Tests

What makes diagnosing ADHD all the more challenging is that, unlike medical conditions like diabetes or cancer, there is no definitive diagnostic test for ADHD. Some physicians administer a brain scan, which can detect differences in brain structure and activity. However, brain differences that are linked to ADHD are also common in head injuries, schizophrenia, and other mental disorders. The tests, therefore, do not provide conclusive answers. For this reason, the American Academy of Child & Adolescent Psychiatry does not recommend imaging tests to diagnose ADHD.

In lieu of medical tests, physicians rely on several different assessment tools. The first is a behavioral history. This involves discussing the patient's behavioral symptoms with the patient and close family members. It also involves gathering written or verbal descriptions of the patient's behavior from current and former teachers, in the case of children. Doctors also use a questionnaire known as the Conners' Rating Scale. Adult patients and their spouses fill it out, and parents and teachers complete it for child patients. The questionnaire helps establish the type and severity of the patient's symptoms. Doctors also take the patient's medical history and administer a medical exam in order to rule out physical problems, such as vision or hearing disorders.

Once the possibility of other illnesses is eliminated, the doctor evaluates the patient's symptoms according to guidelines set in the American Psychiatric Association's *Diagnostic and Statistical Manual of Mental Disorders*. By providing a checklist of symptomatic behaviors and the intensity and frequency of those behaviors, it provides criteria for diagnosing different mental disorders, including ADHD.

One mom describes what happened when her son was diagnosed with ADHD:

> When my son Brian was in second grade, I began noticing that he was increasingly disorganized. It was nearly impossible for him to complete his homework at night, he was antagonistic to his older brother and to his father and to me. . . . Brian couldn't concentrate or focus in class either, especially when he had to complete multi-step projects. He wasn't able to follow his teacher's instructions, and his constant fidgeting distracted his classmates from completing their work. Working together with Brian's teacher and school counselor, we filled out the parent/teacher assessment for ADHD. Armed with my version of the test, I made an appointment with Brian's physician. Brian's doctor spent a lot of time with Brian, and at the end of the appointment he prescribed a pill to treat his ADHD symptoms.[22]

Relief and Regret

Although getting the correct diagnosis is challenging, many people with ADHD say once they are diagnosed they feel as if a great weight has been lifted off their shoulders. Some also feel regret about all the time they lost blaming themselves for their behavior. According to Hallowell and Ratey, "Some diagnoses—like cancer or heart disease—herald the beginning of hard times, but the diagnosis of [ADHD] should mark the end of the worst times and the start of better times."[23]

Treatment with Medication

Once a diagnosis is made, medication is usually the first line of treatment. It does not cure ADHD or eliminate all the symptoms entirely, but it does lessen symptoms in 80 percent of those who take it.

Driving and ADHD

ADHD symptoms can cause problems for drivers. The problem is most pronounced in teenage drivers, who lack the experience and skill of older drivers. Teenage drivers with ADHD are two to four times more likely to get into automobile accidents, three times more likely to be injured, and four times more likely to cause an accident than their peers without ADHD. They are also two to six times more likely to get a speeding ticket and four to eight times more likely to have their driver's license suspended. Their impulsiveness often causes them to drive recklessly, take unnecessary risks, purposefully exceed speed limits, ignore traffic signs, and run traffic lights. Inattentiveness causes them to be less alert to what is happening around them. As a result, they are more likely to veer off the road, not notice brake lights and directional signals on other cars, and respond too slowly to changing road conditions.

Teen drivers with ADHD can overcome these problems. Spending extra time practicing driving with an instructor or family member helps young people succeed as drivers.

Currently, there are two types of ADHD medications. Stimulants are the most common type. These drugs excite or rev up the body. Although it would seem that this is the last thing that people with ADHD need, these drugs have an opposite effect on people with ADHD. They calm them down, decrease impulsiveness, and sharpen their focus. Scientists do not know exactly why this is so. They do know that stimulants cause more dopamine to be released into pathways in the brain. This, scientists say, normalizes chemical imbalances, facilitating the flow of information to the different parts of the brain.

Ritalin, Concerta, and Adderall are among the most common stimulants, but there are a number of others. These drugs are usually taken orally and take effect in about twenty minutes.

A patch placed on the body delivers long-acting medicine. People with ADHD may prefer to use a patch instead of taking pills.

Depending on the particular medication and the dosage, the effects last from three to twelve hours. After this time, any positive effects wear off. Many people with ADHD prefer longer-acting medication since remembering to take medicine can be a problem for people with ADHD.

ADHD medication delivered through the skin directly into the bloodstream is long acting. This medication is administered via a patch that is worn on the patient's body for up to nine hours. Once it is removed its effects continue for an additional three hours. At present, the patch is only available for use by children aged six to twelve. This method of delivery is especially effective for children who have trouble swallowing pills. This form of medication helped Brian, who was first prescribed oral medication to treat his ADHD. According to his mother:

> For a year, Brian tried to take the medication, but it was a challenge every single day because of his aversion to swallowing pills. We hid the pills in everything from yogurt to applesauce, but it was rare that Brian could get the medication into his system. Even on the days he actually swallowed the pill, he sometimes threw it up once he got to school. In sixth grade, Brian [switched to] . . . a once-daily skin patch. We . . . were thrilled with the results.[24]

The other type of medication that can treat ADHD is the antidepressant drug Strattera. It works by elevating the level of norepinephrine in the brain. It does this by keeping the proteins that carry norepinephrine from absorbing any of the neurotransmitter. Strattera, which is taken orally, lasts all day.

Getting the Right Dosage

Prescribing medication for ADHD is not simple. It takes time to determine which medication and dosage best suit a particular patient. If the dosage is too high, patients tend to feel almost sedated; if it is too low, their symptoms do not abate. What makes prescribing the right dosage all the more difficult is that the dosage depends on how fast the patient's body breaks down, or metabolizes, the drug. As a result, it is possible that a young child might require more frequent and larger amounts of an ADHD drug than a grown man. Usually patients are started on the lowest dose of a medication. The dosage is then systematically increased until an effective level is reached.

Moreover, each person responds differently to different drugs. Often patients must switch between medications until they find one that relieves their symptoms without causing other problems. According to Hallowell and Ratey:

> Finding the right dose of the right medicine can take time. It is a process of trial and error, as we do not yet have any tests that can tell us in advance which medication will work best in a given individual or what dose will be the right one. . . . The goal is to get improvement in the negative symptoms like loss of focus or disorganization, without side effects.[25]

According to many people with ADHD, the difference the correct medication makes in their ability to control their behavior is impressive. Ty Pennington puts it this way:

> Bam, it's like somebody gave me glasses and all of a sudden I could see, you know, not only what I couldn't see before but I could see the mistakes I made and how I could correct them [I was] really focusing, my grades went from D's to A's. I'm putting myself through art school. Instead of doing one project, I'm actually completing three, [I] could show how talented I am. . . . Instead of having the idea, I'm actually completing it. . . . I was like, oh my God, this is like the great thing. . . . I was still the guy that would do crazy things but I was accomplishing things I never thought I could. . . . The next thing you know I'm confident.[26]

Medication Can Cause Problems

Despite the help ADHD medicines provide, like all medications, they can cause side effects and present health risks. In the case of stimulants, among the most common side effects is loss of appetite. This can lead to an unhealthy weight loss. Lack of proper nutrition can weaken the immune system and slow growth patterns in children and adolescents. Growth

Stimulants prescribed for ADHD can lead to the development of facial tics, such as winking or blinking.

patterns normalize, however, if treatment is stopped. Even taking breaks from medication, as some young people do during school vacations, appears to help. John recalls:

> My nephew took Ritalin from the time he was five years old until his early teens. He barely ate and was a little skinny kid. In his midteens, he started taking vacations from the medicine. When he was off the medicine, he ate everything that wasn't nailed down. He put on weight, developed some muscles, and got taller. Today, he's no giant, but I'd describe him as an average-sized man.[27]

Stimulants also can cause emotional sensitivity, irritability, headaches, and high blood pressure. Since high blood pressure can lead to heart attacks and strokes, patients who have high blood pressure must be closely monitored if they wish to continue using the medication. In addition, some individuals experience what is known as a rebound effect shortly after the drug's effect wears off. This involves thirty to sixty minutes of increased hyperactivity, impulsivity, and constant talking.

Facial and vocal tics are another problem. Facial tics are sudden, repetitive, involuntary movements, such as winking, blinking, sniffling, lip licking, mouth opening and closing, and head movements. Vocal tics include throat clearing and coughing. Stimulants prescribed for ADHD cause facial and vocal tics in 9 percent of children. Tics can also develop in adults.

Some patients cease taking stimulant medication due to tics. Usually, once patients stop taking the medication, the tics disappear within a few months. But in 1 percent of all cases, tics become chronic.

Some patients counteract tics by taking a drug called clonidine in combination with ADHD medication. Clonidine has its own side effects. If a dosage is missed, it can result in dangerous fluctuations in a person's blood pressure. Blake Taylor explains:

> I took a stimulant medication for ten years: from the time I was five years old until I was fourteen years old. The medication was great and helped me to concentrate and focus, but my tics became progressively worse, and I had

to take clonidine in response. But, as always, there was a catch: if I were to suddenly stop taking the clonidine, whether it was my own forgetfulness or if I had simply used up the pills, my blood pressure could suddenly drop and then rocket back up.[28]

Still another problem is how ADHD medication makes some individuals feel emotionally. They say it changes their sense of self and their personality and inhibits their spontaneity and creativity. Radio and television personality Glenn Beck, who has ADHD, puts it this way:

> If you don't have . . . ADHD, you have no idea what it is like. And when you take medication, it does change the way you think and the way you function. And I was on some medicine, I don't remember even what it was, but I hated it. It totally stripped me of personality.[29]

Strattera poses still other issues. It can cause stomachaches, fatigue, dizziness, nausea, liver damage, mood swings, and suicidal thoughts. In a clinical trial, Eli Lilly, the manufacturer of Strattera, evaluated 2,200 children and adolescents. Strattera was given to 1,357 and a placebo, or sugar pill, was given to 843. There were five cases of suicidal thinking and one case of attempted suicide among the 1,357 taking Strattera compared to none in the placebo group. Although this is a small percentage, the drug does present a risk. As a result, in September 2005, Eli Lilly added a warning to the product's label stating that the medication may cause suicidal thoughts in children and adolescents. For unknown reasons, there does not appear to be a similar risk to adults. Young people taking the drug must be closely monitored. They are advised to tell their health-care provider, parent, or a close relative or friend if they develop suicidal thoughts and to cease taking the medication immediately.

ADHD Medication and Drug Abuse

Still another concern is that Ritalin can be used as a recreational drug because high doses of it produce a euphoric effect.

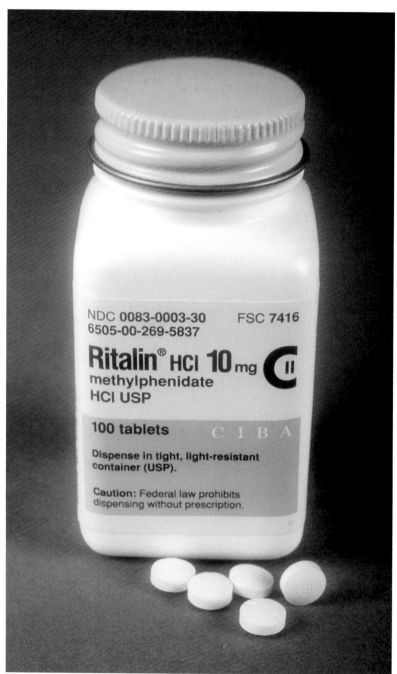

Ritalin, frequently prescribed for ADHD, is a controversial drug because it can have dangerous side effects.

Abusers include young people with ADHD as well as those without the disorder who obtain it from their peers with ADHD. In addition to using the drug to get high, a growing number of young people use it as an appetite suppressant for weight reduction, to stay awake, or to increase focus before athletic events or tests. People who abuse Ritalin call the drug Vitamin R or R Ball.

Large doses of Ritalin can cause serious and even fatal side effects. These include hallucinations, seizures, strokes, dangerously high blood pressure, heart problems, and blood clots in the heart and lungs.

The medications that help ADHD patients with their symptoms are powerful drugs. Finding the right medicine and dosage often takes time, which is worth the effort for patients who eventually find relief. Unfortunately, even when the right treatment is found, some individuals experience unpleasant side effects that make taking the medication difficult or impossible. These patients may seek other types of treatment.

CHAPTER THREE

Other ADHD Treatments

Because drug treatment for ADHD lessens but does not eliminate ADHD symptoms entirely, many people combine medicinal treatment with other traditional and alternative treatments in an effort to further reduce their symptoms. And, since medicinal treatment can cause unpleasant side effects and does not work for 20 percent of ADHD patients, some individuals turn to these treatments in place of ADHD medicine. Like medicinal treatment, other traditional and alternative treatments can present health risks.

Counseling

Talking to a mental health professional is a traditional form of treatment for people with ADHD. It is most effective when it is combined with medicinal treatment. Combining counseling and other forms of mental health care, such as behavioral therapy, with medication to treat ADHD is known as a multimodal approach. It involves a team of people, including the patient, the patient's family, a physician, and a mental health professional.

Counseling helps individuals become more self-aware. During counseling sessions, patients talk about their innermost thoughts and feelings in a safe, nonjudgmental atmosphere.

Children with ADHD can talk with a therapist or teacher about their feelings and the challenges they face.

Many people with ADHD have feelings of anger, frustration, and failure as a result of the disorder. Talking to a counselor allows individuals to discuss these feelings and to learn how to handle them. It also helps them to discover their personal strengths and talents and come up with strategies that use their strengths to cope with the challenges that ADHD presents. Family, work, school, social, and behavioral issues can all be dealt with in this manner.

Counseling comes in many forms and settings. Psychologists, psychiatrists, and mental health counselors all can serve as a counselor or therapist. Therapy sessions can include individual counseling, family or couple's counseling, group therapy, or a combination, depending on what works best for the patient.

Behavioral Therapy

Other types of traditional therapy deal less with emotions and more with behavior. Cognitive behavioral therapy is one of the most common forms of this type of treatment. It is a systematic approach to changing behavior that is especially effective with young children. In this therapy, children learn a set of rules about their behavior and actions. They are taught by using workbooks, talking with mental health professionals, and role-playing. At the same time, the patient's parents are taught the skills necessary to implement the therapy at home.

Patients work at changing one behavior at a time, and their progress is tracked by their parents in the form of a chart or other visual reminder that is displayed in a prominent place in the home. The child earns a gold star or a point on the chart for appropriate behavior. Some parents use a token, such as a button or poker chip. When a set number of symbols or tokens is earned, the child receives a special privilege or reward, such as a small toy or extra playtime. The goals are for children to learn what behavior is acceptable and what is not and for them eventually to

develop enough awareness to monitor their own behavior without the help of a chart or rewards.

Focusing attention on good behavior, rather than negative behavior, helps makes this happen. Experts often advise parents to ignore inappropriate behavior when possible since many children behave badly just to get attention. Teachers can also work with parents by using similar behavioral tactics with the child in school.

Parents can supervise their kids and reward them when the youngsters stay focused.

Yvonne Pennington used behavioral therapy with Ty when he was a child. She explains how it worked:

> For every 10 seconds that Ty managed to stay focused and do as he was asked, he earned a token [in the form of a drink coaster]. Ty was allowed to exchange the tokens for a reward—10 coasters for, say, an extra half hour of TV or time to play with his Erector Set. At first, Ty rarely earned more than a token or two before returning to his usual antics. But . . . Ty's behavior slowly improved, and that gave his self-esteem a much needed boost. In the past people had only paid attention to Ty when he did something wrong. But with the token economy, we turned that around.[30]

Because it is especially difficult to diagnose young children with ADHD accurately, the American Psychological Association recommends using only behavioral therapy to treat children under the age of five. Children over the age of five respond well to a combination of drug and behavioral therapy. According to the National Institute of Mental Health, medication alone, as well as medication and behavioral therapy together, result in the greatest improvement in ADHD symptoms in children. The multimodal approach is especially effective in modifying defiant behavior, as well as improving interactions between children and all other people, including their parents, teachers, and peers.

Alternative Treatments

Counseling and behavioral training are, like medication, traditional treatments for ADHD. They are generally accepted by the medical community in the United States. Other ADHD treatments are less conventional and are not accepted by traditional doctors. These treatments are known as alternative treatments. Some forms of alternative treatment have been widely studied, while some have not. Conventional treatments like medications undergo rigorous testing and must be approved as safe for the public by the U.S. Food and Drug Administration (FDA), the government agency that regulates medicines. Alternative treatments, however, are not regulated by the U.S. government, so using them can be risky.

Despite these concerns, some people with ADHD turn to alternative treatments to help relieve their symptoms. Some patients combine alternative treatments with traditional treatment in a method known as complementary treatment, while others use alternative treatments in place of traditional treatments.

A number of traditional health-care professionals believe that some alternative treatments can be beneficial in treating ADHD, especially when used in addition to traditional therapies. Clinical psychologist and ADHD expert Barbara Ingersoll explains, "Asking if you should use medication or complementary therapy to treat [ADHD] is like asking whether you should eat fruit or vegetables. You often need both."[31]

Herbal Therapy

Herbal therapy is a well-established form of alternative treatment. It uses the stems, roots, leaves, bark, and seeds of plants known to have healing properties to treat any number of illnesses, including ADHD.

A number of different herbs are used to treat ADHD symptoms. These include Saint-John's-wort, ginkgo biloba, vinpocetine, and blue-green algae. Although it is not known exactly how these herbs work, it is believed they contain substances that increase blood flow to the brain, raise levels of neurotransmitters, enhance the activity of neurotransmitters, and/or create a feeling of calm. They are taken in capsule or liquid form, or as a tea.

Saint-John's-wort is derived from the flowers of the plant of the same name. It has been used to treat mental disorders, such as depression, for centuries. Saint-John's-wort seems to work similarly to antidepressant medications. Chemicals in Saint-John's-wort are thought to increase levels of the neurotransmitter norepinephrine in the brain. Some people with ADHD say that Saint-John's-wort makes them feel more emotionally balanced. It calms them down, relieves their anxiety, and lifts their mood. There is no scientific evidence, however, to prove the herb actually has this effect. A 2008 study at Bastyr University, in Seattle, Washington, found that Saint-John's-wort is no more effective in treating the symptoms of children with ADHD than a placebo. Still, many people with the disorder say Saint-John's-wort helps them.

Saint-John's-wort, shown here in various forms, is an herb thought to help a person feel less anxious.

Ginkgo biloba is another popular herb used to treat ADHD. Herbalists say it contains chemicals that increase blood flow to the brain, which appears to enhance a patient's focus and memory. According to two small European studies, another herb, vinpocetine, which comes from the leaves of the periwinkle plant, also seems to increase blood flow to the brain, especially to the frontal lobe, the part of the brain involved in attention and restlessness. In addition, vinpocetine seems to contain a substance that increases dopamine levels in the brain. The herb, which is quite powerful, is currently available as a prescription drug in Europe and Japan, where it is used to treat people with head injuries and strokes and is being studied as a treatment for Alzheimer's disease. It is available in the United States in health food stores. Proponents say it increases mental clarity, improves focus, lessens inattention, and improves memory and concentration.

The water plant blue-green algae is yet another popular ADHD treatment. It is unclear how the plant affects the brain, but it appears to contain proteins that are important to the health of neurons and neurotransmitters. People who take blue-green algae say that it increases their ability to concentrate and reduces restlessness and anxiety.

There are very few studies looking into the effect of blue-green algae on ADHD. A 1995 Nicaraguan study does not focus specifically on individuals with ADHD, but the results are interesting. In this study, a group of 111 school-age children were given blue-green algae every day for six months. During this time, the children's academic performance, class participation,

ADHD and Green Time

Scientists have found that being outdoors in a natural setting improves people's ability to concentrate and perform mental tasks. Using this knowledge, researchers at the University of Illinois at Urbana-Champaign conducted a study in 2007 to see whether spending time outdoors impacts ADHD symptoms.

University researchers had the parents of 406 children with ADHD track their children's weekend and after-school activities and how these activities affected the children's behavior. When the children spent time indoors, their symptoms did not improve. When the children spent time in a natural setting, however, they were less restless and better able to focus their attention, complete tasks, and follow directions. In many cases, the children also slept better at night.

and ability to focus were monitored and compared to that of a control group. Although there was no significant difference between the two groups at the start of the study, after six months the group taking blue-green algae showed significant improvement when compared to the control group. Many people with ADHD say they also notice a marked improvement in their ability to focus when they take blue-green algae.

Without more intense studies, it is unclear whether blue-green algae or other herbal treatments really improve ADHD symptoms. Despite this uncertainty, many people with ADHD say herbal treatments help them. Vicki is one of these people. She explains:

> I have found a natural medication that works very well for me. It slows the brain processes somewhat so that I'm on an even keel with the majority of the population. The doctor that prescribed this medication listened to what I said. . . . I asked him if he had any idea what it was like to have 50 million ideas running through your head at the same time and you can't keep any one of them long enough to think it through to a logical conclusion because you're being bombarded by the other 50 million ideas? We then discussed the benefits of alternative medication. I agreed to try it. The difference the correct medication makes is unreal. I have not had any negative physical side effects. It does not produce a feeling of mental instability or zombie like effect. It is not the medication for all [ADHD] persons, but it is the correct medication for me.[32]

Nutritional Supplements

While some individuals turn to herbs, others find that complementing traditional ADHD treatments with nutritional supplements lessens their symptoms. Omega-3 fatty acid, in particular, appears to have a positive effect on ADHD symptoms.

Omega-3 fatty acid is a healthy fat that strengthens the immune system, helps brain cells develop and function, increases blood flow to the brain, and raises dopamine levels in the brain. The body cannot make omega-3 fatty acid but can obtain it from food or nutritional supplements. It is found in fatty cold-water fish, like salmon, tuna, sardines, and anchovies; nuts and seeds; avocados; dark leafy vegetables; and certain oils. Nutritional supplements include fish oil or flaxseed capsules.

A number of studies show that children with ADHD have lower-than-normal levels of omega-3 fatty acid in their bloodstreams. One conducted in 2008 at the University of Guelph in Ontario, Canada, measured omega-3 fatty acid levels in the blood of a group of adolescents diagnosed with ADHD. The results were compared to the results of another group of adolescents of

Fish-oil capsules are a good source of omega-3 fatty acid, which seems to help lessen ADHD symptoms.

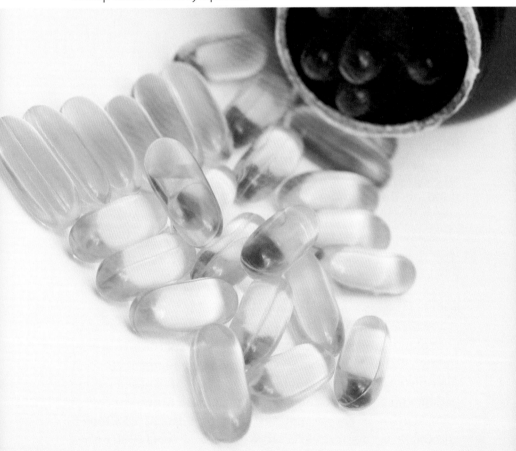

the same ages and weights that did not have the disorder. At the same time, the behavior of each adolescent was rated on the Connors' Rating Scale. Not only did the ADHD group have significantly lower levels of omega-3 fatty acid in their blood than the control group, but there was also a correlation with blood levels and rating scores—the lower the blood levels, the poorer the scores on the rating scale.

It is not known if there is a cause-and-effect relationship between low levels of omega-3 fatty acid and ADHD symptoms. The nutrient has been proven to help those with bipolar disorder, but there is no definitive proof that it relieves ADHD symptoms. However, a number of studies are beginning to confirm that it does. For instance, in a 2007 University of South Australia study, 103 children with ADHD were given either an omega-3 fatty acid supplement or a placebo every day for fifteen weeks. All the children were rated on the Connors' Ratings Scale at the start of the study and again after fifteen weeks. Researchers found that after fifteen weeks the scores of the omega-3 fatty acid group improved in impulsivity, inattention, hyperactivity, and social interaction. In comparison, there was no change in the control group's scores. Both groups were then given omega-3 fatty acid plus a multiple vitamin for an additional fifteen weeks. Once again, all the children were rated on the Connors' Rating Scale. This time every child's scores had improved to such a degree that the researchers concluded that treating ADHD with omega-3 fatty acid is just as effective as Ritalin. Although a few smaller studies in Europe have yielded similar results, other studies have not. For this reason, health-care professionals do not yet recommend substituting omega-3 fatty acid supplements for Ritalin.

However, since omega-3 fatty acid is essential for good health and proper brain function, ADHD experts Edward M. Hallowell and John J. Ratey take omega-3 supplements to treat their own ADHD and recommend it for their patients. "I tell my patients there are two things they need to do for their health," says Ratey, "exercise and consume omega-3s." Hallowell agrees: "It seems to help most with mental focus."[33] He says that it takes about six weeks before patients notice the effect.

Iron and ADHD

Some individuals with ADHD also add more iron to their diet, either by eating more iron-rich foods or by taking iron supplements. Iron plays a key role in the production of neurotransmitters and helps to regulate the flow of dopamine in the brain. Therefore, it is reasonable to theorize that an iron deficiency could lead to a chemical imbalance, which might cause ADHD symptoms. A 2004 University of North Carolina at Chapel Hill study tested this theory. In this study, researchers measured iron blood levels in fifty-three children with ADHD and in twenty-seven without. The iron levels of 87 percent of the children with ADHD were abnormally low, compared to 18 percent of the children without ADHD. The researchers also observed that the children with the lowest iron levels had the most severe ADHD symptoms. Based on these results, the researchers said that "low iron stores may explain as much as 30% of ADHD severity."[34]

Diet and ADHD

Eating certain foods and cutting back on others appear to help control ADHD symptoms. White rice, cookies, cake, sugar, and simple carbohydrates found in processed snack foods, and foods made with white flour break down quickly in the body. They create a quick burst of energy, which intensifies hyperactivity. They also cause a surge in blood sugar followed by a rapid drop. This lowers a person's ability to concentrate and worsens inattention. Complex carbohydrates found in whole grains, beans, and lentils, which break down slowly and do not cause blood sugar to spike, are a better choice.

Eating plenty of protein also prevents blood sugar surges. In addition, protein contains amino acids, which the body uses to manufacture neurotransmitters. Many people with ADHD say that eating a protein-rich diet increases their ability to concentrate and decreases restlessness. Meats, fish, poultry, eggs, beans, seeds and nuts, are all good sources of protein.

Even if low iron levels do worsen ADHD symptoms, it is not known whether taking iron supplements improve them. Some individuals say iron supplements help, but there is no conclusive scientific evidence to prove this. What is known is that eating a diet rich in foods that contain iron is healthy. Such foods include meat, fish, poultry, eggs, whole grains, fortified cereals, legumes (beans and peas), vegetables, and some fruits. Even if these foods do not alleviate ADHD symptoms, they will have a positive impact on a person's mental and physical health.

Are Herbs and Nutritional Supplements Safe?

Many people believe that because herbs and nutritional supplements are natural, they are safe and do not cause side effects. This is not true. Anything that is powerful enough to alter body functions can cause side effects and health risks, including herbs and nutritional supplements.

Herbs contain powerful chemicals. Many are as strong as drugs and like drugs can cause a number of side effects. For example, vinpocetine can cause chest pain, headaches, breathing problems, and stomach upset in some people, while Saint-John's-wort can cause nausea, fatigue, anxiety, dizziness, headaches, and sun sensitivity. Saint-John's-wort can also interact in the liver with certain medications, including antidepressants. This can cause toxic results when chemicals in the liver turn this combination into a poisonous and potentially fatal compound. In fact, it is illegal to sell Saint-John's-wort in France due to herb-drug interactions.

Complicating matters, the lack of U.S. government regulations means herbs do not have set dosages. Therefore, herbal treatment may be weaker or stronger than patients antici-

pate. There have been cases in which herbal remedies have been found to be three times the strength written on the label. This can be dangerous. For instance, ginkgo biloba contains chemicals that thin the blood. High levels of the herb can inhibit the blood's ability to clot and cause dangerous bleeding.

Another problem is that the ingredients in herbal treatments and their purity are not monitored. While the leaves of ginkgo biloba are relatively safe to ingest, the seeds are poisonous.

Many people think that herbal supplements such as ginkgo biloba, shown growing here, are unsafe.

Some species of blue-green algae contain mercury and other toxic contaminants. While most herbal supplements are unlikely to contain these dangerous ingredients, without careful monitoring, there is no way to be sure the herbs are safe. Moreover, since herbal supplements are plants, they can cause an allergic reaction in susceptible individuals.

Nutritional supplements, too, are not without risk. High doses of iron supplements, in particular, can be dangerous. Excess iron is not eliminated from the body. Instead it circulates through the body and can weaken the body and cause disease. High levels of iron are linked to Parkinson's disease, a disease of the nervous system. For this reason, many health-care experts advise patients to get their iron from food rather than from supplements.

No ADHD treatment is perfect. And, alternative treatments are unproven. Individuals with ADHD know this. Yet, despite side effects and health risks, many are willing to try them in order to relieve their symptoms and gain better control of their behavior.

CHAPTER FOUR

Living with ADHD

Living with ADHD presents many challenges. Inattentiveness, disorganization, forgetfulness, impulsiveness, and hyperactivity can cause problems for individuals with ADHD in every area of their lives. By taking steps to cope with these challenges and getting support from others, people with ADHD can be happier and more productive.

Taking Control

Inattentiveness makes it hard for many people with ADHD to organize their thoughts, time, data, finances, and personal possessions. As a result, they tend to lose things, miss appointments, have trouble finishing tasks, and forget to do important things. It is no wonder that they often feel that their lives are out of control.

Disorganization is a real problem for many people with ADHD. The level of disorganization in ADHD sufferers is usually much greater than that of an average person. "Disorganization can plague your soul," explain ADHD experts Edward M. Hallowell and John J. Ratey. "It is one of the great bugaboos in the life of someone who has [ADHD]. We have trouble organizing things. We have trouble organizing time. We have trouble organizing thoughts. We have trouble organizing data. We put things in piles. We put time into limbo as we procrastinate. . . . As inevitably as a match burning, we fall behind. . . . We feel overwhelmed and inept. Incompetent. Lost. And so sad."[35]

Taking steps to add structure to their lives helps individuals with ADHD feel more in control. Many of these steps are identical to those that people who do not have ADHD employ as organizational tools. The difference is that individuals with ADHD depend on these tools more than other people and use them to a much greater degree. Keeping to-do lists and notes and posting them in visible places, like on the refrigerator, is one way people with ADHD remind themselves of what they have to do. "I have to put notes on the front door that I can't miss before I go out so I don't forget anything. When I cook, I write myself a note to make sure I remember I have something in the oven or I'd burn down the place,"[36] explains Ron, a man with ADHD.

Calendars, daily planners, or a device like a personal digital assistant (PDA) are other tools individuals with ADHD can use to manage their time better. Besides recording appointments and deadlines, people with ADHD find it useful to record regular activities, such as picking up a child from school every day at 3:30 P.M. Otherwise, inattentiveness can lead them to forget such routine tasks. People with ADHD also use calendars, daily planners, and PDAs to help break up large assignments into several smaller tasks. This is known as "chunking." It is an effective tool for individuals with ADHD who are often unable to organize their time well enough to complete a large project. In addition, some individuals set timers or alarms on watches, clocks, and PDAs to help keep them on track and remind them of daily tasks. Nancy, a woman with ADHD, says, "I use my cell phone to help keep me organized. I put reminders, appointments, and my work schedule in the phone to help me keep track of where I need to be."[37]

Computers also help. Using a computer instead of writing things down allows individuals with ADHD to keep track of and file important information while minimizing loose papers, which are easily misplaced. According to Blake Taylor, a high school student with ADHD, "You can use a computer to help

For people with ADHD, organizing their time with a PDA can be very helpful.

file and organize your papers and notes. . . . You can take notes on a laptop instead of taking notes by hand. Having the notes on your computer reduces your clutter factor significantly, and so you will become more organized. I have found that buying a laptop was the main way I solved my organization problem at school."[38]

Using a computer to handle personal finances is another step that brings structure into ADHD patients' lives. Computer programs that track finances and automatic bill paying are two measures that help. Since people with ADHD often forget to pay bills or simply lose them, such programs can be a lifesaver.

Coping with Social Problems

Individuals with ADHD often face social problems. Many feel insecure and are afraid that their ADHD behaviors will alienate other people. Many young people with ADHD are teased because of their behavior, which leads them to be distrustful of others. As a result, they sometimes have problems making friends and developing and maintaining relationships.

Even when individuals with ADHD try to make friends, they often fail. Their inattentiveness makes it difficult for them to make eye contact, read nonverbal cues, or be good listeners. Their hyperactivity causes them to fidget while others are talking, and this makes others feel that they are being snubbed.

Attending etiquette classes can help. In these classes individuals are taught how to introduce themselves, have a conversation, and use good manners, among other things. Having these skills helps boost a person's confidence. Special social-skills training classes, conducted by a mental health professional, are similar. They cover topics like making friends, reading body language, and making eye contact. There are also software and books that help teach social skills.

Designating specific areas for things like schoolbooks, keys, and other items that can be easily misplaced is one more strategy that helps. Simple measures like having a hook by the front door for keys, a basket for bills, or a special shelf for schoolbooks or work-related papers help people with ADHD get organized. "If you put something back where it belongs, it will be there when you next need it," says Taylor. "I'm always a little surprised when I put my books on their assigned shelves in the kitchen and then find them there the next morning when I'm stuffing things into my backpack for school."[39]

Exercise Helps

Participating in physical activity is another way individuals with ADHD cope. Exercising focuses the mind and allows individuals to release pent-up energy, which lessens feelings of restlessness. Moreover, exercising for at least thirty minutes causes the brain to release endorphins, natural chemicals that give the exerciser a feeling of well-being.

Like ADHD medications, exercise stimulates the production of dopamine and norepinephrine in the brain, which explains its positive effect on ADHD symptoms. The more vigorous the exercise is, the more powerful the results. Olympic swimmer and ADHD sufferer Michael Phelps trains six to eight hours a day. The effects of his exercise schedule on his ADHD symptoms have made it possible for him to stop taking medication entirely.

Most individuals do not exercise as vigorously as Phelps and, therefore, are not able to replace medication with exercise. But they do find that regular physical activity improves their focus, mood, and problems with restlessness, which helps them to better meet the challenges they face. Physician and author Michael O. Flanagan, who has ADHD, explains, "When I was younger, I relied heavily on exercise to cope with my symptoms. In fact, I had a boss once tell me that unless I exercised before going to work, I shouldn't even bother to show up at all. Without the exercise I was irritable, edgy, and unfocused, but with it I was calm and able to concentrate and get my job done."[40]

Any form of physical activity helps relieve ADHD symptoms. Certain types of exercise, however, which involve movements

In some cases, exercise can help ADHD symptoms almost as much as medication.

that activate areas of the brain that control concentration, focus, evaluating consequences, timing, and sequencing appear to strengthen connections between neurons in these areas of the brain. As a result, scientists theorize that frequent participation in these activities may have a positive long-term effect on ADHD symptoms. These activities include skateboarding, gymnastics, martial arts, skating, rock climbing, whitewater rafting, and ballet.

Other Measures That Deal with Restlessness

Exercise is just one tactic people with ADHD employ to deal with restlessness. Feelings of restlessness make it difficult for people with ADHD to sit through meetings and classes or do their jobs properly. It can be hard for them to watch a movie or have dinner with friends. Seeking out activities that channel high energy and allow freedom of movement is a way individuals cope. This may involve centering social events around activities like dancing or skating rather than sedentary ones like going to the movies.

Combining a physical activity with a mental one also helps. For example, individuals may solve a

White Noise Helps

A 2007 Swedish study found that background noise, or white noise, helps people with ADHD concentrate. In this study, two groups of children, one group with ADHD and the other without, were given tasks that measured their concentration and memory level with and without white noise playing in the background. The researchers found that concentration and memory level improved in the children with ADHD when the white noise was playing. The non-ADHD children, on the other hand, performed better without the background noise. The researchers say that white noise stimulates brain activity and increases dopamine levels. Since people with ADHD appear to have lower levels of dopamine and brain activity than those without the disorder, the effect of the white noise is to reduce ADHD symptoms and to help those with ADHD to concentrate. Individuals without ADHD, on the other hand, already have high levels of brain activity and dopamine. Increasing these levels appears to overstimulate their brains and disturb their ability to concentrate.

Based on the results of this study, some people with ADHD are using white noise to help them concentrate.

problem while jogging, watch television while cleaning house, or pace the room while planning a party. According to many individuals with ADHD, this strategy not only helps lessen restlessness but also helps turn off mental distractions, which improves their focus. This may be why many students with ADHD are most successful in hands-on, project-based classrooms where movement is part of learning.

Channeling energy into accomplishing something is another step individuals take. Cleaning the house, gardening, walking the dog, doing community service work, or playing an instrument, for example, all let individuals release energy in a positive manner. Indeed, a 2006 Massachusetts Institute of Technology study found that musical training helps improve brain functions. Blake Taylor plays the piano as a way to calm his mind and his body. "Classical music," he explains, "is very good. . . . Oftentimes, in the middle of my homework, I will go to the piano to play a Chopin etude or Mozart piano sonata piece. If I am nervous, I suddenly find I can relax and my mind seems better able to focus."[41]

Selecting a career that requires high energy levels is another important step. Doing so allows people with ADHD to turn what appears to be a liability into an asset. Firefighting, law enforcement, acting, construction, teaching, nursing, landscaping, and farming are just a few examples of high-energy jobs.

And, for those circumstances when individuals with ADHD have to remain still, keeping an object handy that they can fidget with can help. One of Hallowell's patients says:

> As a medical student, I spend a lot of time in lectures, studying, and talking to patients. So with all the listening I do, I need something to fidget with. My solution is Silly Putty. I have three eggs of Silly Putty. One egg lives in my book bag, so I can use it when I am in a lecture. One egg lives in the left pocket of my white coat, so I can reach in with my left hand and play with it while I am talking to a

An active career, such as firefighting or police work, can be a good fit for a person with ADHD.

patient and still have my right hand free to take notes, and one egg lives at home on my desk where I can play with it when I am studying. Silly Putty is great. It's easy to un-stick from almost any surface, including fabrics; it's fun to play with, and it's cheap, so if I lose an egg, it's just a dollar to replace it. And because it's roughly the same color as my skin, it's unobtrusive. Silly Putty must have been made for ADDers.[42]

Dealing with Sleep Problems

Physical and mental restlessness and hyperfocusing can cause sleep problems for people with ADHD. When hyperfocusing, people with ADHD forget to sleep. Setting an alarm to go off at bedtime is one strategy that reminds people to go to bed.

Melatonin can help people with ADHD calm down and fall asleep.

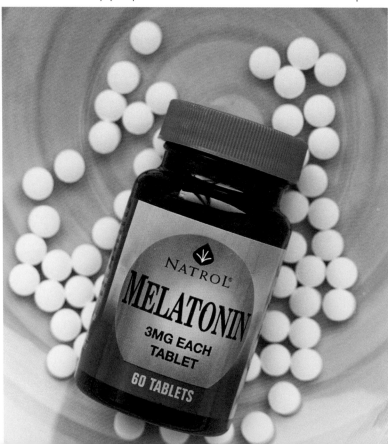

Other measures involve making adjustments in the time of day stimulant medication is taken. Since these medications calm people with ADHD, taking a small dose an hour before bedtime allows many people with ADHD to get to sleep. Taking a sleep aid in the form of melatonin, a chemical that is involved in the sleep process, seems to help many people, too.

Drinking warm milk or eating a protein-rich meal in the evening are other sleep strategies. Both are calming and prevent feelings of hunger, which often plague individuals with ADHD when the appetite suppressing effect of stimulant medication wears off. Keeping the bedroom dark and cool also helps, as does listening to soothing music. Some people listen to CDs of nature sounds designed to give listeners a feeling of calm.

Getting Support

Getting support from others is another way people with ADHD meet the challenges they face. Many turn to an ADHD coach, a specially trained professional whose job it is to motivate and help individuals with ADHD develop and implement strategies that help them to cope with the disorder. Coaches help clients to set up concrete goals and teach them specific strategies to achieve these goals. They collaborate with their clients, monitoring, guiding, and supporting them every step of the way. They support individuals when they fail, analyze why they failed, make suggestions on how to improve, keep individuals from giving up, help individuals to harness their talents, and cheer on successes. ADHD coach Jodi Sleeper-Tripplett, who coached Rob, a teenager, for three years says:

> I was originally hired . . . to help with Rob's academics. It was the usual stuff for kids with [ADHD]. He wasn't into school. Wasn't taking his medication regularly. . . . Part of my role is to coach Rob with making choices, like when to go to a party, when to do homework, how to keep medication on track. Initially, we spent a half-hour on the phone each week. A lot of our focus was trying to improve his organizational skills and time management. . . . What a coach does is put structure down in place for someone whose brain doesn't do it naturally.[43]

Peer Support

Many individuals with ADHD find that joining a support group helps, too. ADHD support groups consist of people with ADHD who share their experiences. Groups can be multiage or consist of just adults or teens. Groups usually meet in public buildings, like community centers, schools, or churches, and are run by a mental health professional or someone with experience or training in working with people with ADHD. There are even Internet groups for people who do not have time to attend meetings physically.

By sharing their common experiences, support group members learn coping strategies for problems that individuals without ADHD do not understand. Support groups also provide members with encouragement and a sense of belonging. Ari Tuckman, who ran an ADHD support group in Pennsylvania,

Some people with ADHD join support groups.

says, "Don't underestimate the power of a support group. . . . Attendees [find] it helpful to tell stories, get advice, and share resources to help them at home, at work, and with friends. A good support group does something that nothing else does—it won't replace an understanding romantic partner or a knowledgeable therapist, but it will complement them nicely."[44]

Children can find similar support in special summer camps for young people with ADHD. Being with children like themselves helps young people with ADHD to feel less isolated and different. This builds their confidence and fosters positive self-esteem. Melissa Bailey sent her eleven-year-old son, Jake, who is often excluded from social activities by his classmates, to an ADHD camp. Going to camp and finding peers like himself helped Jake feel accepted and more confident. According to Melissa, "For the first time he actually made friends. He participated in all sorts of outdoor activities, and came home feeling awesome about himself."[45]

In addition, specially trained staff members work with campers to develop skills to help them cope with their disorder. Through team-building activities, campers learn how to work with others and improve their social and organizational skills. Many ADHD camps also offer academic instruction for children with ADHD who have problems in school.

Legal Support

A coach, a support group, and special summer camps can provide young people with ADHD with many coping skills. But even with these skills, keeping up in school can be a big problem for young people with ADHD. The inability to concentrate, inattention, forgetfulness, disorganization, and restlessness all take their toll, causing many young people with ADHD to struggle and fall behind.

Individuals with ADHD may find help and support through two federal laws, the Individuals with Disabilities Education Act (IDEA) and section 504 of the National Rehabilitation Act (NRA 504). Both laws ensure that students with a disability receive an education that meets their individual educational needs and one that is equal to the education of nondisabled students. Many, but not all students, with ADHD are considered disabled and receive help under these laws. It is up to each individual school district to determine a student's eligibility.

Under these laws, students receive special accommodations and modifications in their education, free of charge. The school, the student, and the student's parents are involved in developing an individualized education plan (IEP) for the student. It establishes educational goals for the student and specifies how these goals will be met while keeping in mind the student's individual needs.

Some students are placed in small special education classes, where there is less distraction and noise and where students receive individualized attention. Others remain in regular classrooms, but modifications are made in order to help the student succeed. These modifications may include more time to complete assignments and tests; shortened assignments; seating in a less-distracting part of the classroom, such as near the teacher and away from doors and windows; allowing students to tape-record assignments and instructions; after-school tutoring; help with note taking; and computer-assisted lessons. According to Taylor, "ADHD is a recognized condition, and you can have a special plan in place, just for you, at school. They call it an individualized education plan, or IEP. The plan lists your skills and talents and the things you need to improve. It also lists what your teachers can do to help you improve. . . . Having an IEP can make all the difference in how successful you are in school."[46]

In the workplace, the Americans with Disabilities Act (ADA) and NRA 504 make certain that disabled workers, including those with ADHD, are not discriminated against and that they are provided with reasonable accommodations. It is up to individuals with ADHD to understand their particular condition well enough to know what accommodations they need. Examples of workplace accommodations include room dividers to lessen distractions, permission to tape-record meetings, permission to wear headphones or use a white noise machine to block out distractions, and being provided with an organizational helper, such as a PDA.

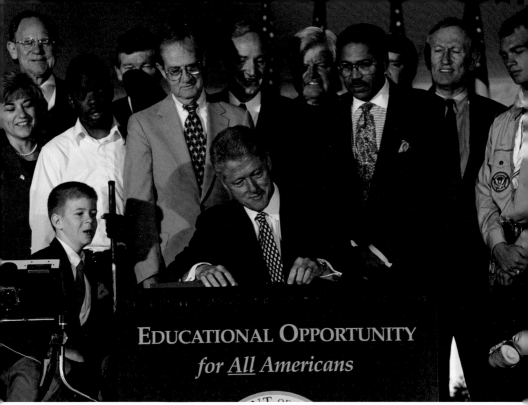

EDUCATIONAL OPPORTUNITY
for _All_ Americans

President Bill Clinton signs the Individuals with Disabilities Education Act in 1997.

Whether at work, at school, at home, or in social situations, living with ADHD is not always easy. By taking steps to add structure to their lives and by getting support from others, individuals with ADHD can be better equipped to meet the challenges they face. In so doing, they gain control over their lives. "Though everyone with ADHD is different," Taylor wisely explains, "we all can gain from taking charge of our individual situation."[47]

CHAPTER FIVE

What the Future Holds

Researchers all over the world are studying ADHD. Some are trying to identify genes that cause ADHD or make individuals susceptible to the disorder. Once these genes are identified, researchers hope to use this knowledge to improve ADHD screening and treatment. Other scientists are looking at new methods of controlling ADHD symptoms.

Pinpointing Specific Genes

In an effort to identify genes common to individuals with ADHD but not to those who do not have the condition, researchers in Europe, South America, Asia, and North America are conducting an ongoing study known as the IMAGE Project. In this study, researchers are analyzing DNA, the chemical code for genes, taken from fourteen hundred families who have at least two children aged seven to eighteen, one of whom has been diagnosed with ADHD. The DNA is extracted from blood samples taken from each family member. It is examined and the different genes found in the samples are recorded. Then the findings are compared. Since most family members share many common genes, the scientists are focusing their attention on whether the children with ADHD carry gene variants or mutations that members of their family who do not have ADHD do not carry and whether other children with ADHD also carry these genes. To provide the researchers with a large pool of information, all the findings are being compiled in a database. This should make it easier to identify genes specific to ADHD. According to Philip Asherson of the Institute of Psychiatry, King's College London, "The idea of the project is to create a resource that can be used both now and in the future to find the genes that cause ADHD. This is an exciting opportunity since the resource will be available to some of the best scientists in the world who wish to find the genes involved."[48]

So far, researchers have established that people with ADHD are more likely than other people to have variants of four genes: the dopamine transporter gene DAT1, which is involved in dopamine transmission, and the dopamine receptor genes SNAP 25, DRD4, and DRD5, which are involved in dopamine production and release. No one gene variant has been found in every child with ADHD, and some of the family members without ADHD carry one or another of these genes. Therefore, scientists do not think that the presence of any of these genes alone causes ADHD. They theorize that the presence of any one of these genes makes individuals more susceptible to the disorder, with susceptibility increasing with the number of variant genes a person carries. According to Asherson, "It is now established that variants of several genes occur more frequently in children with ADHD than in other children. None of these genes are necessary or sufficient on their own to cause ADHD. Rather it is the cumulative effects of several genes."[49]

This is not to say that a specific gene that causes ADHD does not exist, but that if it does, it has not been identified yet. Indeed, with continued study, if there is such a gene, scientists are likely to find it.

Genetic Testing

In the meantime, researchers are using what they have learned to develop a genetic screening test that will establish whether young children carry any of the genes that make individuals susceptible to ADHD. Although such a test will not conclusively predict that a child will develop ADHD, it will show whether the child has a predisposition toward the disorder. This knowledge would allow the child's parents to take steps to minimize the severity of the disorder before symptoms arise. These steps include implementing behavioral therapy techniques, providing opportunity for physical exercise, and teaching the child structuring strategies. University of California at Los Angeles ADHD expert Susan Smalley says, "We believe that once we can identify children at risk for ADHD prior to the onset of symptoms we can help 'tailor' environments to minimize impairment and maximize the strengths of the ADHD child, adolescent, and adult."[50]

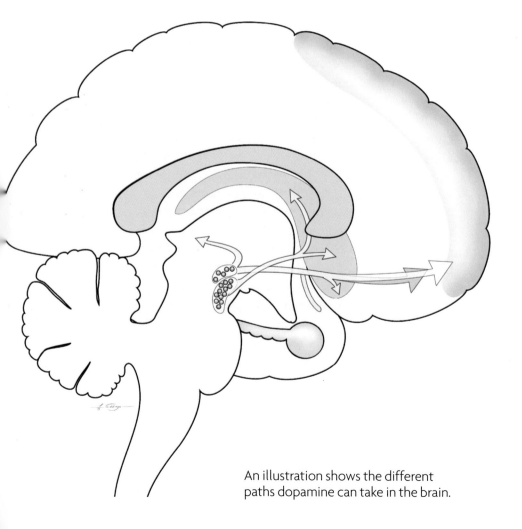

An illustration shows the different paths dopamine can take in the brain.

At present, three companies have developed genetic tests for mental disorders. The tests are marketed on the Internet. Patients send a spittle sample or a swab of the inside of the cheek to the testing company. Scientists who work for the company look for genes linked to different disorders. Then, the company sends the patient a report of what was found. These tests are expensive and not well regulated. Their accuracy is questionable. Scientists are working on developing cheaper, more precise tests.

Genes and Treatment

Currently, the methods for determining the right medication and dosage for individuals newly diagnosed with ADHD are imprecise. Genetic testing should help. A 2008 study at the University of Illinois used genetic tests to predict the effectiveness of ADHD medication. In this study, researchers focused on two dopamine transporter genes known as 9R and 10R. Individuals carry either a 9R or 10R gene, but not both. The researchers used genetic testing on forty-seven children aged five to sixteen with ADHD to see which gene each child carried. Once this was determined, the researchers divided the children into two groups, those with the 9R gene and those with the 10R gene. Then they gave both groups varying doses of Ritalin and tracked how the drug affected the children.

The scientists found that the children with the 10R gene responded well to Ritalin. In contrast, the drug did not significantly improve the symptoms of the children with the 9R gene. Scientists do not know why. They think that something about the 9R gene prevents individuals from responding to Ritalin. To learn more, scientists are conducting a larger study. In it they are focusing on how children with the 9R gene respond to other ADHD medications.

Other scientists are looking at genetic tests that identify genes that determine how fast or slowly chemicals known as enzymes in the liver break down ADHD medications. If individuals carry genes that produce enzymes that break down the medication slowly, they will have higher-than-expected levels of the drug in their bloodstream, which increases the possibility

Scientists perform genetic tests in their search for the cause of ADHD.

and severity of side effects. Conversely, if individuals carry genes that produce enzymes that break down the medication rapidly, they will have lower-than-expected levels of the drug in their bloodstream. Therefore, the drug will not be effective. Knowing how fast patients break down ADHD medication will help physicians determine the appropriate dosage for patients more easily.

Using genetic testing to determine how an individual will react to medication or a particular dosage is not yet a common practice, but scientists hope it will be in the future. This will take away a lot of the guesswork in ADHD treatment. According to University of Illinois head researcher Mark Stein:

> Pharmocogenetics [the study of how genes and drugs interact] has great promise in ADHD, since the effects of medication range from a dramatic positive effect in many individuals while a minority display side effects or do not respond. Since ADHD often runs in families, it seems likely that genetics may play a large role in predicting medication response. But we're not yet at the point that we can use these findings in clinical practice. The hope is that eventually we can identify someone who is likely to benefit from a specific dose or at risk of having a severe side effect who could be treated more successfully with a different treatment approach. . . . It would be tremendous if we could scientifically predict medication response or non-response prior to treatment.[51]

Neurofeedback

Since treating ADHD based on the presence of specific genes is still in the future, some scientists are developing treatments that can help people with ADHD right now. These treatments are based on brain science. One of the most promising is neurofeedback.

Neurofeedback is a process that trains individuals to change their brain activity. Individuals with ADHD appear to have lower-than-normal brain activity. Brain activity is measured in brain waves. The brain produces different types of waves. Those involved in concentration and attention create the most

Brain Waves

There are four kinds of brain waves. All are measured at different frequencies or speeds. Delta waves have the lowest frequency and produce the least brain activity. They exist at a frequency between 0 and 4 hertz, or cycles, per minute. Individuals produce delta waves when they are asleep. At frequencies up to 8 hertz, theta waves are slightly faster and produce slightly more brain activity. They are produced when people are in a relaxed or meditative state.

Alpha waves are produced when people are in a relaxed but alert state, such as when individuals watch television or read a magazine. They exist at frequencies up to 12 hertz. Beta waves, at 12 to 30 hertz, are the most active and fastest brain waves. They are emitted when individuals are in a focused and attentive state. People with ADHD appear to have too much theta activity in their brains and not enough beta, which corresponds to a lower-than-normal level of brain activity.

brain activity. Researchers theorize that through neurofeedback therapy, people with ADHD can learn to consciously produce the brain-wave patterns associated with focus.

To do this, patients are given various mental tasks to perform while electrodes are attached to their head. The electrodes, which pick up electrical signals produced by brain-wave activity, are connected to an electroencephalograph, a machine that records the signals. The signals are then sent to a computer with special software that creates a color-coded pattern similar to a graph. A mental health professional analyzes the pattern and then presents the patient with a series of exercises that helps increase brain activity. These exercises are made up of various video games, which require users to focus their attention in order to win the game. For instance, one game features an airplane that will only fly when players produce the appropriate brain waves.

Scientists theorize that with neurofeedback therapy, individuals will learn what it feels like to focus and will be able to consciously change their brain activity in real-life situations. According to authors Jeff Strong and Michael O. Flanagan, "By repeatedly achieving the desired balance of different types of brain activity, the brain learns to establish the conditions that support those new states, thus making a different way of functioning more likely."[52]

A number of studies have been conducted to investigate the effectiveness of neurofeedback on people with ADHD. A 2006 University of Montreal study looked at how neurofeedback affected attentiveness and brain activity. In this study, twenty children aged eight to twelve with ADHD were divided into two groups. One group was given neurofeedback therapy for thirteen weeks. The other group received no treatment. None of the children took medication for ADHD during the study. The attentiveness of each child was rated one week before the study began and one week after it ended, using input from parents and the results of computerized attention tests. Brain scans were also administered while the children were taking the computerized attention tests. The first scans and attention ratings showed low brain activity and poor attentiveness in both groups. The second showed increased brain activity and attentiveness in the neurofeedback group, but not in the control group. According to Duke University research scientist David Rabner:

> This study supports important new evidence to support the use of neurofeedback as a treatment for ADHD. . . . Improvements for treated children . . . provide a stronger basis for suggesting the neurofeedback treatment was helpful. Most compelling of all, however, is the finding that neurofeedback treatment was associated with changes in brain activation detected by MRI scans. . . . Proponents of neurofeedback treatment have long suggested that it produces enduring changes in brain functioning, and it is these changes that cause ADHD symptoms to diminish. Results from this study provide important initial evidence consistent with this hypothesis.[53]

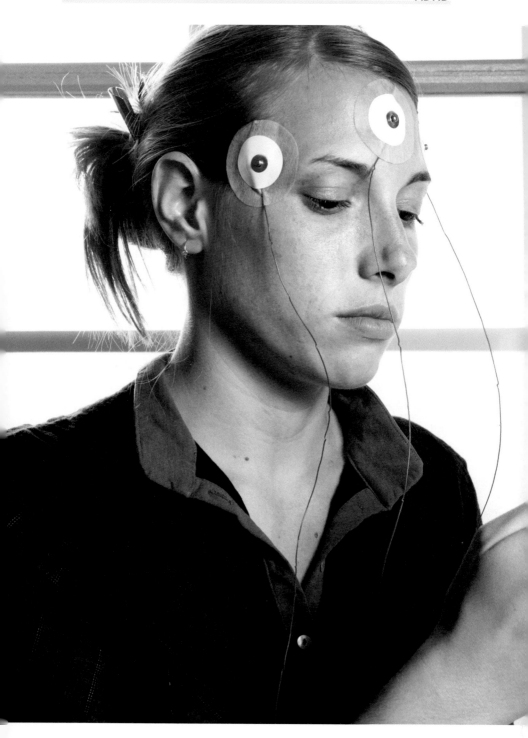

Scientists can measure brain activity with electrodes connected to an electroencephalograph.

Despite these results, the effectiveness of neurofeedback on ADHD symptoms has not yet been proven conclusively. Larger studies with more children and long-term follow-up are needed before it is known for sure if neurofeedback is a successful treatment. Scientists hope to conduct such studies soon. In the meantime, neurofeedback therapy is available through alternative treatment practitioners. If future studies go well, it could become another source of traditional ADHD treatment in the future.

Mental Exercises

Researchers in Sweden are focusing on other ways of training the brain. They have developed a mental exercise program that helps individuals with ADHD improve their working memory. Working memory is the ability to retain several facts or thoughts long enough to use them to solve a problem or accomplish a specific goal. In a broader sense, working memory allows individuals to use past events as a reference for dealing with current events. This helps them plan physical movements, regulate emotions, and organize their thoughts and surroundings.

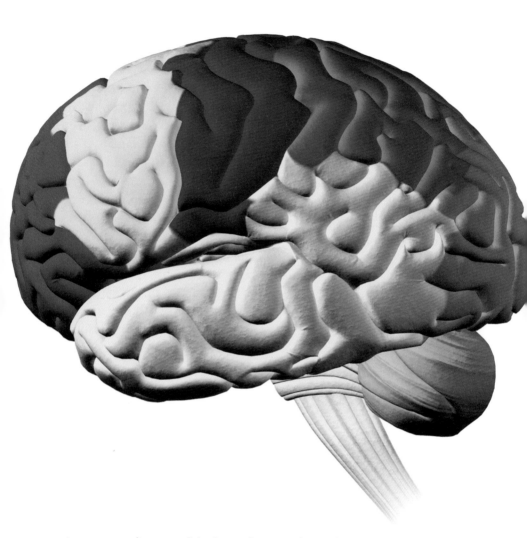

A computer diagram of the brain showing the prefrontal lobe (far left) in purple.

Scientists theorize that people with ADHD have a deficit of working memory. Lead researcher Torkel Klingberg of the Karolinska Institute in Stockholm says that such deficits in individuals with ADHD "can explain why they forget the internal plan of what they are supposed to do next, or forget what they should focus their attention on."[54]

Therefore, the scientists theorize, improving working memory makes individuals more attentive and better able to solve problems. To train working memory, individuals are given increasingly more challenging computer-based mental exercises designed to improve attention. The exercises look and sound like video games. Individuals follow different exercise programs based on an assessment of their working memory. The exercises include activities that involve remembering and repeating words, numbers, or a sequence of events. The more events, words, or numbers trainees recall, the greater the number of items the trainees are holding in their working memory. The training is intensive. It takes place five days a week for an hour a day for at least five weeks.

A 2005 study at the Karolinska Institute tested the effectiveness of working memory training on fifty-three children with ADHD who were not taking medication. At the start of the study, the children's working memory was evaluated via their performance on a span board, a device that tests visual and spatial memory. Then, half the children were given a CD of working memory exercises based on their individual working memory ability and told to work on the exercises every day for twenty-five days. The remaining children served as controls. Both groups were retested on the span board after twenty-five days and again three months after the study ended. The working memory group's scores improved significantly after twenty-five days. The improvement remained when they were retested three months later. The control group showed no improvement.

Moreover, an MRI of each child's brain taken at the start and end of a similar Swedish study showed physical changes in the training group's prefrontal lobe. It is the region of the brain most involved in thought and attention. Once again, these changes were not noted in the control group.

Working memory training is currently available from a company called Cogmed. Other companies are working on developing similar programs. David, a twenty-year-old man with ADHD, says that working memory training helped him. Before he started the training, he was working at a concession stand for the summer. Because of his disorder, it was difficult for him to work the cash register and remember incoming orders. He frequently made the wrong change and confused the orders. Once he started the training, his memory gradually improved. By the end of the summer, he was able to do his job without making as many mistakes. As a result, he became more self-confident. Moreover, a year later, David says he still continues to benefit from the training.

About 75 percent of individuals who receive working memory training show improvement. Eighty percent of these individuals maintain their working memory gains for at least one year, with the level of improvement varying.

Stimulating the Cerebellum

Other scientists are looking at a different form of exercise. They are investigating the effect of physical exercises that involve balance on ADHD symptoms. Such exercises stimulate the cerebellum. The cerebellum mainly controls movement and balance. However, a part of the cerebellum connects to the prefrontal lobe. Scientists think that, at these connection points, the cerebellum is involved with the prefrontal lobe in learning, planning, and judging time. If, they theorize, the cerebellum could be stimulated, brain activity in this area of the cerebellum could be increased. This would help people with ADHD to learn, plan, and manage time better. A 2005 Harvard University study that compared brain activity of children with and without ADHD found that the children with ADHD had less brain activity in their cerebellum while doing a working memory exercise than the children without the disorder.

To stimulate the cerebellum, researchers have come up with exercises that involve the use of a balance board. While standing on the board, exercisers are asked to juggle, move their eyes from side to side, and stand on one leg, among other exercises. Exercisers are instructed to perform the exercises twice a day for ten minutes at a time for at least six months. Such exercises, according to ADHD experts Edward M. Hallowell and John J. Ratey, "draw upon the ability to balance, coordinate alternating movements, and perform actions that cross the midline of the brain and back again."[55] These seem to

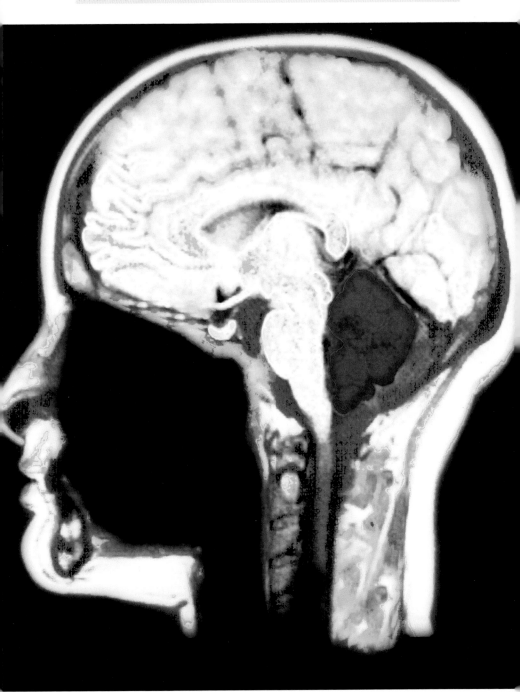

Stimulating the cerebellum, shown here in red, offers promise as a future treatment for ADHD.

Successful People with ADHD

Having ADHD does not prevent individuals from achieving their goals. There are people with ADHD in all walks of life. In an effort to help and inspire others with the disorder, many well-known people have publicly acknowledged that they have ADHD.

One of the most famous of these people is Terry Bradshaw, a sports announcer and a former quarterback for the Pittsburgh Steelers. Other famous athletes with ADHD include Chris Kaman of the Los Angles Clippers; Olympic gold medalist Michael Phelps, a swimmer; and Olympic gold medalist Cammi Granato, an ice hockey player. Granato says that her high energy level has helped her succeed in ice hockey.

Justin Timberlake, Britney Spears, Howie Mandel, Solange Knowles, and Steven Spielberg are also well-known celebrities with the disorder.

Paul Orfalea, the man who started Kinkos, is another famous individual with ADHD. Orfalea attributes much of his success to the disorder. He says that it allows him to think differently than other people. David Neeleman, the founder of Jet Blue Airlines, says that having ADHD made him a risk taker, which helped him succeed.

develop coordination and train the parts of the brain to work together, improving reading, attention, and organization.

A number of small British studies have tested the effect of cerebellum stimulation exercises on learning. None of the studies focused specifically on people with ADHD, but rather looked at the effect of the exercises on people with various learning difficulties, including ADHD. A 2004 study, which was conducted in public schools in Bedfordshire, England, compared the academic performance, behavior, and attentiveness of thirty-six students with learning difficulties who practiced the exercises for a year to students without learning difficulties who did not practice the exercises. At the start of the study, 60 percent of the exercise group exhibited ADHD symptoms. Both groups were evaluated with various tests before the study began and after it ended. The exercise group showed greater improvement in all areas than the nonexercise group. Moreover, at the close of the study, no one in the exercise group exhibited ADHD symptoms. More studies are currently being conducted. If the results are promising, cerebellum stimulation exercises may become a popular ADHD treatment option in the future.

Scientists around the world are working hard to learn more about ADHD. They are using this knowledge to develop new treatments and screening tools that are helping people now and promise to help even more in the future.

Notes

Introduction: A Misunderstood Condition

1. Quoted in PharmaManufacturing.com, "Ty Pennington's Extreme Makeover: FDA Edition," October 3, 2008. http://community.pharmamanufacturing.com/content/ty-penningtons-extreme-makeover-fda-edition.
2. Cassy, "Cassy's Story," Living with ADD, 2007. www.livingwithadd.com/stories/2007/cassy_add_adhd_story.htm.
3. Ty Pennington, interview by Glenn Beck, *Glenn Beck Program*, July 22, 2008. www.glennbeck.com/content/articles/article/196/12741/?ck=1.
4. Allen, "Allen's Story," Living with ADD, 2007. www.livingwithadd.com/stories/2007/allen_add_adhd_story.htm.
5. Quoted in Keath Low, "Kathy," About.com. http://add.about.com/od/themanyfacesofadd/p/kathy.htm.
6. Maya Bolton, "My Liberating—but Late—ADHD Diagnosis," *ADDitude*, February/March 2006. www.additudemag.com/adhd/article/947.html.
7. Quoted in Maureen Connolly, "Struggling with ADHD: I Almost Didn't Make It Through High School," *ADDitude*, August/September 2004. www.additudemag.com/article/852.html.
8. Edward M. Hallowell and John J. Ratey, *Delivered from Distraction*. New York: Ballantine, 2006, p. xxxiii.

Chapter One: What Is ADHD?

9. Hallowell and Ratey, *Delivered from Distraction*, p. 23.
10. Quoted in University of Rochester Medical Center, "ADHD Is 'Real,'" University of Rochester Medical Center. www.urmc.rochester.edu/encyclopedia/content.cfm?pageid=P09010.
11. Jack Prey, "My Battle with ADD," *ADDitude*, August/September 2007. www.additudemag.com/adhd/article/2551.html.

12. Rob, telephone interview with author, July 25, 2008.

13. Bolton, "My Liberating—but Late—ADHD Diagnosis."

14. Julia, personal interview with author, May 16, 2000.

15. Blake E.S. Taylor, *ADHD & Me*. Oakland, CA: New Harbinger, 2007, p. 26.

16. Quoted in PriMed Patient Education Center, "A Lifetime of Distraction." www.patienteducationcenter.org/aspx/Health ELibrary/HealthETopic.aspx?cid=L1004a.

17. Quoted in MedicineNet.com, "Learning Disabilities." www .medicinenet.com/learning_disability/article.htm.

18. William Dodson, "ADHD Sleep Advice—End Bedtime Battles!" *ADDitude*, February/March 2004. www.additudemag .com/adhd/article/757.html.

19. Quoted in Laura Willingham and Patricia Quinn, "ADHD in the Family Tree," ADHD Moms, September 2008. http:// weber10.webprnet.com/omn/ADHD-Moms-Sept-Monthly Feature.pdf.

Chapter Two: Diagnosis and Drug Treatment

20. Greg, "Greg's Story," Living with ADD, 2008. www.living withadd.com/stories/2008/greg_add_adhd_story.htm.

21. Quoted in Bonnie Cramond, "The Coincidence of Attention Deficit Hyperactivity Disorder and Creativity," National Research Center on the Gifted and Talented, March 1995. www.borntoexplore.org/adhd.htm.

22. Quoted in Daytrana, "Daytrana Patient Stories: Brian's Story." www.daytrana.com/Consumers/AboutDaytrana/Day tranaPatientStories.aspx.

23. Hallowell and Ratey, *Delivered from Distraction*, p. 178.

24. Quoted in Daytrana, "Daytrana Patient Stories: Brian's Story."

25. Hallowell and Ratey, *Delivered from Distraction*, p. 81.

26. Pennington, interview by Glenn Beck.

27. John, personal interview with author, October 14, 2008.

28. Taylor, *ADHD & Me*, p. 61.

29. Pennington, interview by Glenn Beck.

Chapter Three: Other ADHD Treatments

30. Quoted in Judy Dutton, "ADD Parenting Advice from Michael Phelps' Mom," *ADDitude*, April/May 2007. www .additudemag.com/adhd/article/1998.html.
31. Quoted in *The ADDitude Guide to Alternative ADHD Treatment*. New York: New Hope Media, 2008, p. 2.
32. Vicki, "Vicki's Story," Living with ADD, 2007. www.living withadd.com/stories/2007/vicki_add_adhd_story.htm.
33. Quoted in *ADDitude* Editors, "The Facts About Fish Oil," *ADDitude*. www.additudemag.com/adhd/article/3334.html.
34. Quoted in Erica Lesperance, "Diet & ADHD: Are There Links Between ADHD & Diet?" Diet Channel, October 4, 2006. www.thedietchannel.com/Diet-and-ADHD.htm.

Chapter Four: Living with ADHD

35. Hallowell and Ratey, *Delivered from Distraction*, p. 328.
36. Ron, personal interview with author, August 14, 2000.
37. Quoted in Keath Low, "Nancy's Story, A Personal Account of Adult ADHD," About.com, November 1, 2006. http:// add.about.com/od/adultperspectives/a/nancy.htm?p=1.
38. Taylor, *ADHD & Me*, p. 41.
39. Taylor, *ADHD & Me*, p. 42.
40. Jeff Strong and Michael O. Flanagan, *AD/HD for Dummies*. Indianapolis: Wiley, 2005, p. 226.
41. Taylor, *ADHD & Me*, p. 54.
42. Quoted in Hallowell and Ratey, *Delivered from Distraction*, p. 312.
43. Quoted in Connolly, "Struggling with ADHD."
44. Ari Tuckman, "ADDA Support Group Manual," Attention Deficit Disorder Association. www.add.org/help/pdfs/Sprt GrpManual07-07.pdf.
45. Quoted in Phyllis Hanlon, "*ADDitude*'s Complete Guide to ADHD Summer Camps," *ADDitude*, April/May 2005. www .additudemag.com/adhd/article/837.html.
46. Taylor, *ADHD & Me*, p. 114.
47. Taylor, *ADHD & Me*, p. 163.

Chapter Five: What the Future Holds

48. Philip Asherson, "The Genetic Investigation of ADHD and the IMAGE Project," BBC. www.bbc.co.uk/sn/tvradio/prog rammes/horizon/adhd_genes.shtml.

49. Asherson, "The Genetic Investigation of ADHD and the IMAGE Project."

50. Quoted in *ADDitude*, "UCLA to Conduct Genetic ADD Research," *ADDitude*. www.additudemag.com/adhd/article/583 .html.

51. Quoted in University of Illinois Medical Center at Chicago, "Study Finds Genes May Predict Response to ADHD Medication," news release, March 2005. http://uillinoismedcen ter.org/content.cfm/adhd_genes.

52. Strong and Flanagan, *AD/HD for Dummies*, p. 177.

53. David Rabner, "New Controlled Study Shows Neurofeedback Helps Children Pay Attention and Improves Their Brain Functions," Peak Achievement Training. www.peak achievement.com/Default.aspx?PageID=1966808&A=Search Result&SearchID=244114&ObjectID=1966808&ObjectType =1.

54. Quoted in Keath Low, "ADD and Working Memory: Pump It Up! Working Out Your Working Memory," About.com, September 15, 2008. http://add.about.com/od/researchstudies/ a/workingmemory.htm?p=1.

55. Hallowell and Ratey, *Delivered from Distraction*, p. 229.

Glossary

antidepressant: A medication used to treat depression.

anxiety disorder: A mental disorder that causes people to be overly worried.

attention deficit disorder (ADD): The name formerly used for attention-deficit/hyperactivity disorder (ADHD).

basal ganglia: The part of the cerebrum involved in motor control, emotions, and learning.

behavioral therapy: Techniques used to change behavior.

bipolar disorder: A mental disorder characterized by periods of great happiness alternating with periods of depression.

brain scan: An image of the brain that is produced with various imaging devices.

cerebellum: The part of the brain involved with movement.

cerebrum: The part of the brain involved with thought.

chemical imbalance: Abnormal levels of neurotransmitters in the brain.

chunking: Breaking up large tasks into several smaller ones.

conduct disorder: A mental disorder that causes individuals to exhibit antisocial behavior.

depression: A mental disorder characterized by feelings of sadness.

dopamine: A neurotransmitter.

frontal lobe: The part of the cerebrum most involved in thought, focus, attention, and impulse control.

gene: Part of a cell that provides inherited information.

herbal therapy: Treatment with plants believed to have medicinal properties.

hyperactive: To be overactive.

hyperfocus: State of attentiveness in which all outside stimuli are blocked out of the mind.

learning disability: A problem in learning that is not caused by low intelligence or poor teaching.

magnetic resonance imaging (MRI): An imaging device that uses radio waves to produce an image of the brain.

multimodal approach: A treatment approach that uses a variety of techniques.

neurofeedback: A process through which individuals learn to control brain activity.

neuron: A brain cell.

neurotransmitter: A chemical that transports information to the different areas of the brain.

norepinephrine: A neurotransmitter.

omega-3 fatty acid: A nutrient found in fish, nuts, and some oils.

schizophrenia: A mental disorder in which people withdraw from reality.

stimulant: A medication that causes the user to feel mentally and physically alert.

working memory: The ability to retain several facts or thoughts long enough to use them to solve a problem or accomplish a specific goal.

Organizations to Contact

Attention Deficit Disorder Association (ADDA)
15000 Commerce Parkway, Ste. C
Mount Laurel, NJ 08054
(856) 439-9099
e-mail: adda@add.org
Web site: www.add.org

ADDA provides information, a blog, a weekly newsletter, and all the latest news on ADHD.

Attention Deficit Disorder Resources
223 Tacoma Ave. S., Ste. 100
Tacoma, WA 98402
(253) 759-5085
Web site: www.addresources.org

Attention Deficit Disorder Resources provides information and support for ADHD.

Children and Adults with Attention-Deficit/Hyperactivity Disorder (CHADD)
8181 Professional Place, Ste. 201
Landover, MD 20785
(800) 233-4050
Web site: www.chadd.org

CHADD offers a wealth of information and support for individuals with ADHD and their families.

Living with ADD
31 Home Depot Drive, Ste. 215
Plymouth, MA 02380
(888) 827-2944
Web site: www.livingwithadd.com

Living with ADD offers information on ADHD, links, lists of coaches, coping strategies, and personal stories.

For Further Reading

Books

Christine Petersen, *Does Everybody Have ADHD? A Teen's Guide to Diagnosis & Treatment*. New York: Franklin Watts, 2007. This is a young adult book covering many aspects of ADHD, including personal success stories.

Alvin Silverstein, Virginia Silverstein, and Laura Silverstein Nunn, *The ADHD Update*. Berkeley Heights: NJ: Enslow, 2008. This is a young adult book dealing with all areas of ADHD.

Blake E.S. Taylor, *ADHD & Me*. Oakland, CA: New Harbinger, 2007. In this book the author, a teenage boy, humorously talks about his life with ADHD and gives tips on how to cope.

John Taylor, *The Survival Guide for Kids with ADD and ADHD*. Minneapolis: Free Spirit, 2006. This is a guide that gives lots of tips and strategies to help young people cope with ADHD.

Periodicals

Ann Barkin and Sandy Fertman Ryan, "Out of Focus," *Girl's Life*, August/September 2006.

Karen Kasland, "Green Time: Unplug and Unwind Outdoors," *Current Health 2*, September 2007.

Nancy Shute, "ADD Brains Might Need More Growing Time," *U.S. News & World Report*, November 12, 2007.

Internet Sources

KidsHealth, "ADHD" http://kidshealth.org/teen/ dieases_conditions/learning/adhd.html.

National Human Genome Research Institute, "The ADHD Genetic Research Study at the National Institute of Health and the National Human Genome Research Institute." www.genome.gov/10004297.

National Institute of Mental Health, "Attention Deficit Hyperactivity Disorder." www.nimh.nih.gov/health/topics/attention-deficit-hyperactivity-disorder-adhd.

National Institute of Neurological Disorders and Stroke, "Brain Basics." www.ninds.nih.gov/disorders/brain_basics/know_your_brain.htm.

Web Sites

ADDitude (www.additudemag.com). This is the online version of the magazine *ADDitude*. It offers personal stories and a wealth of strategies to help people with ADHD.

Addresource.com (www.addresource.com). This site provides information about ADHD and offers lots of links.

ADD/ADHD Support Site (www.attentiondeficit-add-adhd.com). This Web site offers information about causes, treatment, and diagnosis of ADHD; ADHD summer camps; coping skills; and much more.

OneADDPlace.com (www.oneaddplace.com). This site offers support, information, and news about ADHD, including information about famous people with the disorder.

Index

Picture Credits

About the Author

Barbara Sheen is the author of more than forty books for young people. She lives with her family in New Mexico. In her spare time, she likes to swim, walk, exercise, garden, and cook.